WHY FOOTBALL
MATTERS

ALSO BY MARK EDMUNDSON

Why Teach?

The Fine Wisdom and Perfect Teachings of the Kings of Rock and Roll

The Death of Sigmund Freud

Why Read?

Teacher

Nightmare on Main Street

Literature Against Philosophy, Plato to Derrida

Towards Reading Freud

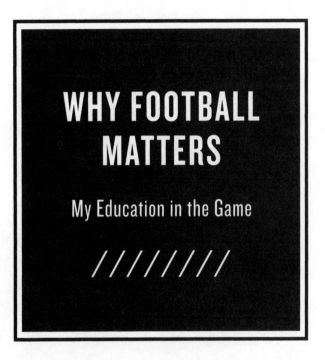

WHY FOOTBALL MATTERS

My Education in the Game

///////

Mark Edmundson

The Penguin Press | New York | 2014

THE PENGUIN PRESS
Published by the Penguin Group
Penguin Group (USA) LLC
375 Hudson Street
New York, New York 10014

USA · Canada · UK · Ireland · Australia
New · Zealand · India · South Africa · China

penguin.com
A Penguin Random House Company

First published by The Penguin Press, a member of
Penguin Group (USA) LLC, 2014

ISBN: 978-1-59420-575-0

Printed in the United States of America
1   3   5   7   9   10   8   6   4   2

Designed by Lauren Kolm

Why Football Matters is a work of non-fiction. Some names and identifying
details have been changed. Any resulting resemblance to persons
living or dead is entirely coincidental and unintentional.

CONTENTS

WHY FOOTBALL
MATTERS

INTRODUCTION

SONS AND FATHERS

I grew up watching football with my father. Starting when I was six years old, maybe seven, I watched Sunday games with him in our cramped apartment on Main Street in Malden, Massachusetts. It was 1958, 1959. We rooted for the New York Giants.

My father loved getting ready for the game. He pushed his king-dad's chair into the middle of the living room, sat down, and tested it. Fine! Then he was up to work his hassock into place and to get his side table where he wanted it. He placed his smokes—Camels, non-filters—on the tabletop along with his matches and his ashtray. "My cigareets," "my asheltray," he called them. Who could say why?

My father was always on the move. He worked two jobs—both at restaurants, both eight-hour shifts—and when he got home from the second one, at the Chuck Wagon, he needed to pace for an hour or two before he could get to sleep. But on Sunday, game day, he calmed down, a little. For my father dearly loved the New York Giants. He loved Gifford and Patton and Katcavage and Robustelli and Modzelewski and Grier and sometimes he loved Sam Huff. All week he looked forward to Sunday afternoon when the Giants came on live.

King-dad chair centered, hassock in place, side table set up: My father was ready to watch the game. But hold it, there was one more thing! His chocolate bar! Every Friday, payday, when my mother shopped, she bought my father a king-size Hershey's chocolate bar with almonds. My father relished that candy bar. He ate it slowly, deliberately, savoring it through the course of the game. He took a nibble, chewed delicately, stared off into space, then looked with sweet gratitude at his Hershey's bar for being as wonderful as it was. The chocolate bar! He gave orders. I ran to get him his Hershey's bar and sat down by his feet and waited for the game to begin.

Then came the music, the NFL theme, piping through the massive body of our black-and-white TV set. My father, who had a wonderful ear, began to sing in wordless harmony. Football was about to begin! To my mother, who was working in the kitchen, cleaning up the Sunday dinner, which my father had cooked, he issued one of his favorite lines: "Hon," he said in a tone of mock tenderness, "they're playing our song!"

And then we watched football. Or at least we tried to. The picture was black-and-white and the reception sometimes miserable. During certain games I had to stand up, go over to the TV, and monkey with the antenna. My father gave commands. No, no. Work the rabbit ears. Flatten them out. No, no, no: straight up, straight up. No, no, no, no: three o'clock. Not nine o'clock, three. As I moved the ears, my father crouched closer to see the next play. Sometimes his nose nearly kissed the screen.

"I think that you're just going to have to hold it there!" A human hand wrapped tight around the aerial could sometimes improve the picture, bringing it from sandstorm in the desert to cloudy day near home. So there I would stand, hand clasped around the aerial, staring into the screen, tilting my head almost upside down, looking into the action, with my glasses sliding down the bridge of my nose. "That's a little better," my father would say. "That's almost good."

But mostly I was spared the acrobatics and contortions; mostly my father and I sat and watched football together. Through football my father explained the world to me. And in time he made me want to play. I wanted to be like the guys on the screen, the heroes, the mythical men. Even then I knew it was a ridiculous wish. I was big enough, but I was soft and fat and good at school. I wore glasses. I was last kid picked, or next to last.

My father believed in almost no one. He disliked politicians: He called John F. Kennedy, who was then our senator, Black Jack. He had no time for newspaper writers or big-name authors. He never went to church, never opened a Bible, and never said a word about God. He thought his bosses were fools. In time he came to love Johnny Carson—and Richard Nixon too. But when I was a small boy, football players were the only men my father admired. He loved Jim Brown and he loved Yelberton Abraham Tittle, Y. A. Tittle.

As much as my father adored his New York Giants, he still loved it when Jim Brown got on a roll against them. To my father, Jim Brown was the greatest football player ever—there never was one like him; there never would be. When Brown stepped on the field my father's love for the Giants dissolved. (Sam Huff, their fierce linebacker, became "Huff the Bluff.") Then the game was all about Jim Brown. Play after play Brown took the ball and plunged into the middle of the line. For a moment everything was still; there was an unmoving knot of snarling, pushing men. But then the pile moved—not much; a foot, maybe. Almost miraculously—it didn't seem like he'd been touched—a Giants player flew off the front of the mass. "There goes Huff!" And then another Giant came off, faster this time, like an electron shot into space. The pile broke and New York Giants, and a few Cleveland Browns, scattered like crumbs. Staggering slightly, alone in what had been the middle, was Jim Brown. He was free and he was pumping down the field for ten, twelve, fifteen more yards, until a couple of defensive backs hopped on him from behind and a couple of the linemen who had been shaken off the pile managed to get up and get downfield and there were finally four or five Giants on him. It took that many men to tackle Jim Brown.

Jim Brown: nine years in the game, set and kept the career rushing record for more than three decades, until he was surpassed by a player who had been in 50 percent more games than he had. Jim Brown: gained more than five yards per carry, an astonishing feat. In theory, if you simply gave Jim the ball every play, you would get a first down in only two attempts. There would be no third down drama. Jim Brown had the feet of a ballerina when he dodged tacklers or skipped along the sidelines, but he had the muscle of a bull. He never ducked a hit: He ran over his enemies. When he finally was tackled, he rose with slow dignity. (Brown called it "getting up with leisure.") "He's like a king out there," my father said. "He's a king!"

When Brown was on one of his rolls, carrying the ball play after play, it was like watching a powerful fighter land blows on a heavy bag—except as he landed the blows, the bag crumpled; the bag caved in. That was the other team, that caving bag. Brown seemed to play with no furor, no hatred for the opposition—though who could know what he felt inside? He simply did what he did. Sometimes my father was in such awe of Jim Brown's performance that he called my mother from the kitchen and said, "Hon, you gotta see this. Lookit, lookit, lookit this!"

My father was teaching me something then, and it was about grace and toughness and manly dignity. This was what it meant to be a man, a formidable man who played with fierce confidence and, when his helmet came off, spoke with sureness and modesty. You could tell that Brown was intelligent and thoughtful, but more than that he brought an aura with him: an enhanced sense of being, a glow.

A lot of the neighborhood dads admired Jim Brown. I'd been at my friends' houses during games and I knew, though some of them were so loyal to the Giants that they couldn't give number 32 all he deserved. But in other houses, I heard something else too. There I was reminded that Jim Brown was a black man, and sometimes I was reminded in ways that were less than decent. My neighborhood was reasonably tough, working class (though far from a slum), and full of hard-edged Irish and Italian guys. "Look at that jungle bunny go!" "Man, that nigger can fly!" Years later, when I was watching a Patriots game, a Boston defensive back intercepted a pass and ran it back over half the field for a touchdown. My friend's father whooped with delight: "Put a tail on him. Put a tail on him and put him back in the jungle. Look at that little monkey go!"

I heard stuff like that all the time, but never from my father. My father probably didn't know more than a few black people—he was friends with a beat cop who'd been a star athlete at Malden High, Harold Jay, and he worked with a few black guys at his restaurant jobs. No racist word ever passed his lips, at least in my hearing or my brother's. He was the only white man I knew well that I could say this about. My father looked at Jim Brown as a fellow human being who had been born with gifts and then gone on to develop them and achieved a level of excellence that had to inspire awe. Lookit! Lookit! Lookit!

Watching football brought my father out of his frustrations and resentments and let him feel true admiration. Watching the game liberated him. In most of life he was irritable, prone to harsh judgment. But not when he was watching football; then he was another sort of man. He saw something greater than himself on the screen and he loved it—and he tried to teach me to do the same.

———————

The football-watching ritual meant a lot to me, and one day my father showed me that it meant something to him too. My father was usually generous with his chocolate bar. At any time during the game I was free to ask, "Dad, can I have a piece?" He knew that I didn't care for the bullet-like almonds inside the bar, so he crafted me a piece of pure chocolate. I could ask again, especially if the Giants were doing well, or if Jim Brown was running his thoroughbred race up and down the field. But I had probably better not ask three times.

One Saturday morning I crept sock footed into the pantry and found the bar on a top shelf. I slid it down, opened the wrapper, smelled the intoxicating scent of chocolate—my father had told me that the whole town of Hershey, Pennsylvania, smelled that way, and I wanted to go there and get a dose. Then I broke a piece of pure chocolate out from between the rocky almonds and dispatched it. Why was this so bad? My father always gave me a piece of chocolate during the game. Today I was taking payment in advance. Come to think of it, my father almost always allotted two pieces of almond-free when a contest was on.

By Sunday morning of game day the chocolate bar was no longer a chocolate bar. It was a collection of chocolate-covered almonds inside a crumpled, clumsily secured dark wrapper. The chocolate-covered almonds were not attractive, no. They were misshapen and sharp edged: They looked like black rocks.

Game time came, the game began, and my father, for whatever reason, did not call for his chocolate bar. (My father loved to call for his amenities. When I hear the Christmas carol about Old King Cole and how he "called for his pipe and he called for his bowl, and he called for his fiddlers three," I think of him.) Was he doing this to torture me? Did he know? When he was angry my father did not hold back. He roared. If I didn't scram fast enough, he delivered a whack.

I had been tempted to recite my chocolate sin in confession that Saturday and receive absolution for it. But by two o'clock, when I was kneeling in front of the priest in the confessional at the Sacred Heart, the chocolate bar was still semi-intact and might have been passable. And even I recognized that there was a certain absurd ring to "Bless me father for I have sinned. My last confession was one week ago. Since then I have lied three times, sworn twice, fingered the almonds out of my father's chocolate bar, and eaten a lot of the rest."

At halftime my father called for his bar. I went to its hiding place and drew it down, opened the wrapper, and laid the wreckage out. Then I walked to the living room. I put the remains before my father with both my hands. I looked at the mess, and without a word, took it and placed it on the tray table beside his ashtray and his smokes ("asheltray"; "cigareets").

At the second-half kickoff he picked an almond and popped it in his mouth and chewed thoughtfully. The second half went on, my father, consuming his chocolate-covered almonds, intent on the game but unusually quiet. Most of the time his word count overwhelmed the announcer's. It was usually a landslide victory, Wright Edmundson over Chris Schenkel. I sat in silence, waiting for the storm.

Early in the fourth quarter—the Giants well in the lead and Jim Brown off terrorizing the Redskins or the Eagles—my father made his move. A hand dropped down in front of my face—a fist, really—and I jumped. Now it was coming: the holler, the clout, the tearful run to my bedroom. But the hand opened. In front of me was a bit of chocolate, a mite but completely almond-free. "You missed a piece," my father said.

My father loved Y. A. Tittle, maybe even more than he loved Jim Brown. When he watched Jim Brown he felt that he was watching a deity. Brown had thrown himself into the crucible of the game and emerged as something like a man-god. But he had begun with amazing gifts. There was only one way to regard Jim Brown, and that was by looking up.

With Tittle it was different. With Tittle it wasn't a matter of awe—Lookit! Lookit!—but of something else. Tittle was an artist of the gentle, perfect pass, dropped into the receiver's hands like a soft Wonder Bread loaf from the sky. The ball floated toward the spot and at exactly the right moment it descended to Gifford or Jimmy Patton, who scattered away like he'd swiped it off the shelf. Tittle had a big arm and could boom the ball down the field when he wanted to, but to my father Tittle—or YAT, as he sometimes called him—was an artist of the perfect short, soft pass.

My father's response: I could catch that! Even I could catch that! My father's pass catching credentials were modest. He had been a track star in junior high school. For a while the neighborhood kids had called him Flash. In high school, he had done some high-speed maneuvering on foot to evade various pursuers, some of them, I gathered, in blue. But an athlete he was not. When we began watching football he was only about thirty years old, but a steady training table diet of fried food, cigarettes, and a few beers (three to ten) whenever the opportunity naturally arose and sometimes when it didn't had taken most of the run-and-jump out of him. Occasionally he'd chase me around the park in a game of one-on-one football, but in three or four minutes he'd collapse on a concrete bench mumbling about cutting back a little on his smokes. (This was the era when doctors touted cigarettes in ads on the pages of major magazines. They said that tobacco was highly relaxing.) My father did sometimes quit. Quitting is easy, he said, I've done it a half-dozen times.

My father was no athlete. But still he said, "I could catch Tittle's passes." "Do you think so?" I asked him. I was truly interested. When I was very young my father told me stories about his past adventures. These often took place in the old west and featured encounters with Indians and various desperadoes. He had, I learned, a long-running feud with Geronimo, the fiercest of the Southwest chiefs. A few times, my father had been ambushed by Geronimo and his braves. At least once, my father had been captured. After being adopted into the tribe, he had escaped, making his way to Malden, Massachusetts, in time to marry my mother and to sire me. I asked multiple questions about how he had managed this feat. But I almost fully believed his stories—I was four or five at the time. I believed them enough to share them with my friends in the neighborhood, whose fathers, it turned out, had not fought heroically in the Indian wars of the Southwest. The neighborhood reaction, when it came, got my father to tell me that we should probably keep the Geronimo-fighting phase of his life to ourselves. It was a while, though, before he stopped telling these stories, and of course I continued to believe them, more or less.

When my father said that he—even he—could catch one of Y. A. Tittle's passes, I took him seriously. And when he said at least once that I probably could too—well, that was information I filed away. Over time, my father came to believe that he could maybe throw some of Tittle's passes. Not the longer ones when he really showed his stuff, but the puffballs, the floating dandelion heads, that Tittle dropped over the line of scrimmage and that went for big gains.

My father talked all the time about Tittle. He wasn't long on talent; he wasn't a born star. (My father would have appreciated the title of Tittle's autobiography: *Nothing Comes Easy*.) Tittle had made himself a great Giants quarterback by hard work and by applying his intelligence. The intelligence was key. The man knew the game. He had worked to develop a feel for who would be open, and when. Tittle looked a little like a wizard too, with his hawk eyes and his bald head. (We kids remarked on how many pro football players seemed to be bald. Our explanation?

They took too many showers. The blasts of hot water blew the follicles out of their heads.) My father could play ball? Maybe (maybe, maybe) I could do it too. Football wasn't only a game for nature's aristocrats, like Jim Brown. (Jim Brown had about the same assessment of Tittle as my father did. "He reminded me of an old truck—didn't sound good, didn't look good, kept on crossing that desert while all those pretty new cars were stuck on the side over-heated.") So why not me?

Football was a game you could succeed in by being smart and tough and dedicated. And maybe my father implied something more there on Main Street in Malden, a town founded by Puritans, people who believed in work of the hand and work of the spirit. Was it possible that you could make yourself into a man like Y. A. Tittle? Could somebody who really threw himself into football—or any other important endeavor—give a new shape to himself? Could you become another sort of being, a better one, through the exercise of intelligence and will?

I was good at school. But I was soft and weak and credulous (those Geronimo stories!), and I was dreamy. I was one of those kids who sit by the window for hours watching the dust float down through the shafts of light—dreaming, dreaming. My mother and father loved me; that was plain enough. But they surely feared that the world might be too much for me if I didn't get a little tougher, a little stronger.

My mother talked to me about Teddy Roosevelt, who, like me, wore glasses and liked to read and had asthma. He was sickly as a boy, my mother told me. But he was determined to make something out of himself. He worked out with weights in the gym; he swam and ran and he camped outside and rode horses. (I asked for a horse. No dice.) He became a soldier and the president and he wrote books.

I'm not sure my father ever saw the famous photograph of Y. A. Tittle, perhaps the best-known black-and-white shot of an NFL player ever taken. Tittle is kneeling on the ground, dazed; he's clearly been knocked there and knocked hard. His helmet is off and there's blood running down his face. He looks alone and confused and he even looks afraid. He has the presence of an old general who's completely lost the day. His troops have been scattered by the forces of an upstart and he's about to be thrown in chains and wheeled off in the cart.

He's overreached himself, the photograph says. He's pushed his luck and his modest skills too far. He's not only defeated; he's self-defeated. This is a guy who has risen as high as he can go, but that rising has given him a long way to fall. What he's seeing and feeling has got to be the dark side of this game. He's tasting the brutality, the hard animal cruelty of football. It's possible that what happened to Tittle that afternoon stayed with him. Headaches, dizzy spells, and memory loss—they all may have arisen from that blow and others like it that he took in his career.

I didn't know it at the time, watching games with my father there in Malden. How could I have? Football has a dark side too. It gives and it also takes away, and often it does both at once.

But in Malden, Massachusetts, around 1960, I had no room for such thoughts. I saw Jim Brown, a man who began with amazing gifts and then put them to work. And my father taught me to see in Tittle a man who had made himself into more of a man. (I didn't know it and I doubt my father did, but like me and Teddy Roosevelt, Tittle suffered from asthma.) And this I remembered. This I took to heart.

My football education began with my father. Of how many other boys in America, past and present, is that true? I might even say that my education proper, my education in the ways of the world, began with watching football with my dad. And how many others might say the same—both for better and for worse?

We're told repeatedly that football is America's game. It's a main source of entertainment—maybe *the* main source in our culture. And it's big business too: billions of dollars a year. But football is more than business and entertainment. For millions who play, or have played, football is a form of education. We Americans invented this complex, violent, beautiful game—we shaped it. But the game shapes us too. It shapes us when we play and after we've turned in our pads for the last time. It shapes us while we're in it and then later when knowingly or not we take what we've learned from the game out into the world.

It's not just a guys' issue, though guys are most immediately engaged. More and more, women are going to be getting involved. Some will play, sure. (One recalls with pleasure that the first well-known girl high school football player was named Elizabeth Balsley.) But women—mothers and aunts and grandmothers and friends—are going to be getting more engaged in the decisions about whether the boys in their lives will play or not. It used to be almost a given: If a boy wanted to play football, then he played. No more. After revelations about head injuries and other harm that can come from the game, more women are going to feel compelled to decide about football. And I suspect many will be seeing it as a form of education. Are the virtues a young guy can acquire playing football worth the risks? And what precisely are those virtues; what exactly are the risks?

The coaches will tell you that football can develop character, stir courage, enhance manliness, and cultivate patriotism, faith, and loyalty. The game can teach you how to win and, maybe more important, how to lose. I believe that what they say is so. But football's virtues come with risks. The game has a dark side. The character that football instills can lead to dull conformity; the bravery it cultivates can in an instant turn brutal. Football engenders loyalty to the team, but the loyalty too often devolves into a herd mentality: my fellow players, right or wrong. Football endorses faith and patriotism. But is football really a Christian game if "Christian" means conformity with the teachings of the Gospels? Football can prepare young people for the military. But the game may also idealize soldiering and war in ways that can be fatally misleading. Brutality, thoughtlessness, dull conformity, love for the herd mentality and the herd—these can be products of football too.

We need a deeper understanding of the game than the one the coaches, boosters, and broadcasters offer. We need to recognize how much football can give, yes: The game can be a superb school for body, heart, and mind. But we also need to see how much harm football can do, and not just to the body. Football is a potentially ennobling, potentially toxic school for the spirit. When you play the game seriously, you put your soul on the line.

"Be a football player!" we Medford Mustangs used to chant after our toughest drill, running up and down a steep bank we called the Pit. We yelled the words loudly, with pride. We were high school kids. "Be a football player!" But I doubt that any of us—least of all me—really knew what we were saying.

I

EARNING A UNIFORM:
CHARACTER

At the first installment of Medford Mustang two-a-day sessions, I looked around me in the locker room and saw what must have been a hundred other guys all in white practice outfits. I was among a strange new tribe, but I surely didn't feel part of it. I was disoriented and anxious, and I hated being inside my pads. I could hardly move. It felt like someone had locked me down in a set of rusted chains. I had imagined that the uniform would give me a boost, the way a suit of armor must have done for a young knight. I'd hoped that, padded and fitted out and standing in the room with the stars of last year's unbeaten Greater Boston League champs, I'd feel like a warrior among warriors.

When I first told my friends that I was going out for the team, they didn't believe me. They thought I was lying when I said that I'd be going to the stadium soon to pick up pads and then begin two-a-day practices. But then they saw I was serious, and they could hardly contain themselves. It was absurd that someone with my deficits should step on the field with the high school idols.

I was a junior in high school then, a buttery, oversensitive boy, credulous and shy. (I hadn't changed all that much from the too-tender kid who'd watched football with his dad on Sundays ten years before.) I'd never been much of an athlete. I wasn't usually the last picked in the school yard now, but sometimes I was close. I surely wasn't the sort of kid the gym teacher spots and commands to go out for the football team. I was probably a touch depressed too, though that wasn't a term we used in Medford, Massachusetts, in 1968. (We'd moved to Medford from next-door Malden when I was thirteen.) A couple of my friends actually laughed in my face when I told them about my plan. I'd taken a few steps toward going out for the lowly sophomore team the year before, then gotten sick: colds, asthma, infections. To my (so-called) friends, that was even more reason to doubt me.

What was I doing going out for football? Why was I trying to join the team that the year before had gone undefeated and won the Greater Boston League title? I'd always been drawn to the game and happy to play at the park. Slow as I was, I loved running with the ball. Heavy as I was, I wasn't always easy to tackle. But this wasn't going to be a slapdash affair with my buddies. Now I was placing myself under the iron law of the coaches. I'd be blocking and tackling in ways that scared me to think about.

But there were no doubt deeper reasons for me being in that locker room with all those guys tricked out in white on that first day. Somewhere in me there had to be the memories of Sunday afternoons watching football with my father. Somewhere there must have been the image of Jim Brown, the perfect football player and perfect man. But more important were surely memories of Y. A. Tittle, the guy who had built himself up a brick at a time. I needed some building up then—I needed it badly.

The equipment room was depleted when I got in to pick up my pads early the morning of the first day. I was one of the last guys through. The stars from last year's varsity team came first, next were the players from the sophomore squad, and last were the kids you might have called walk-ons. These were the guys who had no playing experience in the Medford High football system. Even the walk-ons came into the equipment room in the order of what the coaches took to be their promise. I was one of the last.

On the first day of practice we stood in ten or so military lines, captains up front, and we began doing exercises. They were basic calisthenics: jumping jacks and squats and a few push-ups (not many). In a T-shirt and shorts I could have handled them fine. But in the uniform they were murder. I felt like I was pushing a boulder up a hill and the boulder would hardly budge. In twenty minutes I was sweating from all pores, my face was tomato red, and my muscles felt frayed and ready to quit. My feet hurt because my cleats didn't fit; my hands were filthy; I thought I'd pulled a groin muscle. Practice hadn't actually begun.

"How do you move inside this stuff?" I asked the guy next to me as we jogged to our first drill. If he answered I didn't hear him. But in not too long a scrimmage began and the guy taught me how to move in pads. He did it by flying at me while he was blocking on a sweep and knocking me half-senseless. Everybody laughed. One more down! He's had it. He'll quit.

During the first days of double sessions, other players struggled against their rivals for starting positions. They fought to impress the coaches. They strove for status in the locker room. They went after what warriors from the start of recorded time have wanted: the first place. "Who is going to be Stud of the Line?" John Kelly, the guard and linebacker coach, would holler. He was the right guy to pose the question. He'd earned the power to designate players as studs, aspiring studs, or hopeless losers. He was about six feet tall, absurdly handsome, with a black fleece of curly hair. He looked like the actor Elliott Gould, except he looked better. If he said you were Stud of the Line, you were Stud of the Line.

Kelly's favorite diversion was to oppose Victor Guest (Guestie) and Tommy Lyons (the Brain). Victor was a good student and a squared-away guy, about six feet three and 220 pounds; he said yes sir and he said no sir and he was going to college. The Brain was called the Brain in the same spirit that a guy in a motorcycle club who weighs 350 pounds and whose butt melts over the side of his saddle like pudding is called Tiny. Tommy would probably not be going to college. His face looked like someone had cracked a bottle across it. He was smaller than Guestie and probably not as strong, but as for the perennial football question—not how big is the dog in the fight, but how big is the fight in the dog?—the answer wasn't hard to come by. Guestie's father wanted him to play football; various war gods wanted Tommy in the game. Kelly loved getting the two going head-to-head to see who might on a given day be Stud of the Line.

During the opening days of double sessions, Guestie and the Brain battled with each other to see who was Stud. John Anastasio and Stan Ingalls fought to see who would be starting quarterback. John was a fine athlete but couldn't always remember the plays. Stan was good on the plays, but was prone to getting his feet tangled with the center's after the snap.

All this manly competition went on far over my head. I was struggling with the heat and the drills and the hitting. And I was having a major war with my pads.

Would I make it? Many days during double sessions I thought about quitting. I wouldn't have to roll out of bed at six in the morning and stumble down to the bus stop to get to practice; I could forget the calisthenics and the tackling drills (where I was often humiliated) and stop coming home so tired that I passed out after dinner. I could probably get a whole night's sleep, rather than waking up at three in the morning with a leg cramp that made me scream. (The remedy for this? My father flew into my bedroom and screamed at me to stop screaming.) And I would never have to put on my miserable pads again.

That year the coaches were united in their belief that drinking water on the practice field was dangerous. It made you cramp up, they told us. It made you sick to your stomach, they said. So during practice, which went on for two and a half hours, twice a day, during a roaring New England summer, we got no water.

Players cramped up, anyway; players got sick to their stomachs, regardless. Players fell on their knees and began making soft plaintive noises; they were helped to their feet and escorted to the locker room.

The coaches didn't cut anyone from the squad that year. Kids cut themselves. Guys with what appeared to me to be amazing athletic talent would after a few two-a-day practices walk hangdog into the coaches' locker room and hand over their pads. The coaches rarely tried to encourage them to stay. If a kid couldn't take it, he couldn't take it. There was no water to be had on the field and there were no compassionate fatherly talks.

There were simply the two-and-a-half-hour practices twice a day, each of which ended with grass drills. We formed ranks and ran in place; when the coach blew the whistle, we jumped up, spread-eagled in the air, and went bang facedown onto the hard ground. He blew the whistle; we got up and started again. Some guys went bang and stayed on the deck panting, which meant that they had to quit. They brought their dirty practice uniforms home, had them washed by their mothers, and the next morning gave them to the coaches in white, fresh-smelling bundles like loaves of home-baked bread. When I asked one guy why he quit he said simply, "I couldn't take it."

Could I? There was little reason to think that I could. I was doughnut soft around the waist, nearsighted, a slow runner, and not quick at all. It turned out that underneath the soft exterior I had some muscle and that my lung capacity was well developed, probably from the bouts of asthma I'd had as a boy, when

I'd fought for air like a long-distance runner. And of course I had those Sunday afternoons watching football with my father. I had what he'd told me about Jim Brown and about Y. A. Tittle.

Sometimes after morning practice I was so dazed that it took me an hour to shower and get dressed. By the time I was in my street clothes, the locker room was often empty. A few times I wasn't sure that I would be able to find my way to the bus stop to get home, so I went below the bleachers and fell asleep, woke up two hours later, hiked to a convenience store to buy what passed for a lunch, and then dozed off under the stands again. By four o'clock, when the other players were returning, I was in front of my locker, dressing in slow motion. Soon I was on the field, ready to go. I cried in my sleep one night at the thought that the next day I would have to go back to practice.

Could I take it? My uniform with its heavy pads was an ongoing affliction. I'd never known myself to be claustrophobic, but when I put the uniform on I felt like someone had shoved me into a closet, turned out the light, and locked the door. There wasn't much air in the closet and I had to strain for breath. I wasn't going to suffocate; it wasn't that bad. But I felt confined, bound up. I couldn't hear well from inside the helmet and I had trouble seeing past my face guard. (The better, more experienced players usually had complex cages. My face guard was virginal white plastic and looked like someone could break it by grabbing on and twisting hard.) The big pads were saddlebags on my shoulders; the knee and thigh and girdle pads made me feel like I couldn't lift my legs, much less run.

When I tried to move in my pads I was a mechanical man with a blazing short in his circuitry. There I was, grinding down, falling apart. Watching me run wind sprints, the coaches would sometimes crack up laughing. "Are you running or doing the boogaloo?" Kelly asked me on one particularly bad day early in double sessions. Laughter rose from all directions—when Kelly made a joke, that joke was funny.

Sometimes I wanted to pull the coaches aside and explain, "It's the uniform, dammit. It's the pads." I wasn't a track star when I ran in T-shirt and shorts, but I could get from one place to another without provoking mirth. I had no future in ballet, but when I walked around my house, I could keep my balance and refrain from knocking the ashtrays over. But put me in pads and I was a stumbling half-drunk guy. Damn, did I hate that uniform!

But I loved it too.

One day during double sessions, I took my uniform home, pads and all. When no one was there in our apartment I pulled it on. The shoulder pads and thigh pads; the pants that once washed and bleached were so tight that I had to jump into them; the hand pads and forearm pads that I'd gone out and bought with my own none-too-plentiful funds—I got it all on. It took twenty minutes. I skipped the cleats; my mother would have hated what they'd have done to the floor. Then I made my way into the bathroom and turned on the blazing white light overhead and closed the door. On the back of the bathroom door was a full-length mirror.

I got into the linebacker crouch, the way Kelly had taught me to do. My back was arched, legs bowed, arms presented in front of me, with the padded forearms—the "flippers," as Coach called them—flourished. I reenacted the hit-and-shed drill. I did a jab step with the left foot and shot the right forearm ahead— quick, controlled, hard, aimed to pop the top of the offensive guard's helmet and make it ring inside as though a madman was yanking the bells high in the cathedral tower. Step and pop, step and pop, step and pop: It was a simple dance. I did my forearm dance, and I was practicing; yes I was. I'd need to make a move five thousand times at home in preparation for making it half successfully on the field.

Generally the mirror and I weren't on agreeable terms with each other. I'd gotten my nose from my father—pronounced; my chin from my mother—recessed; and a scattering of zits from wherever it is they come from. (I believed pizza to be the culprit, but couldn't stop eating the stuff.) Usually when I passed a mirror, or a plate-glass window, or even the windshield of a car, I did what I took to be a subtle duck-and-cover. But with my uniform on, it was different.

I fixed myself in the linebacker crouch and tensed my body and stared hard through my nearsighted eyes at the being in the mirror who looked to be part man, part machine. That guy seemed pulled together and strong. That guy looked like he knew something. He was someone you didn't want to mess with.

The next day I went back onto the field and the guy in the mirror was nowhere to be found. I was back doing the short-circuit robot. When you can't get yourself going all in the same direction at a respectable clip on a football field, you're in trouble. You become a fat target for anyone on the other side of the ball. On a sweep, the blocking back caught sight of me shambling toward the ballcarrier, drew a bead, and closed. When the contact came, I offered no real resistance: I flew in every direction, as though I'd been detonated from inside. Tremendously satisfying for the blocking back—who was much smaller than I was. And it was danger-free. I was too disordered to hit back. "Get low! Get low!" the coaches screamed. I tried and I tried. But in those early days of practice I was sending signals to my body that it couldn't process. So kaboom! Rick Marciano, who was so small I could have bench-pressed him, blew me up.

Would I make it? Could I survive the ten-day double-session ordeal? Probably not, if I couldn't figure out how to maneuver inside my pads. It was a matter of time before someone knocked me flat and put me out for the season. Or before the coaches decided enough was enough and that there was one guy, just one guy, they needed to cut.

I kept trying. Every day of double sessions I put on the pads and did the drills and jumped in on defense when the first string had the ball. (I was a real jumper-in.) The coaches told us that we needed to give it 100 percent all the time. Most of the players knew that there were times to push and times to let up. Not me. I gave it everything all the time, which made me so tired by the final half hour of practice that I had trouble standing. But in the long run it was making me stronger. And when you're sixteen years old you can gain strength fast. Gradually, I was getting accustomed to the armored state that some of my fellow ballplayers seemed to have been born used to.

One day toward the end of the ten murderous days of double sessions, I caught a break. We were running wind sprints at the close of practice, wind sprints prefatory to the hated grass drills. I was not running the wind sprints with much distinction, even though it was only guards and tackles, slow guys, in my group. (I was a guard on offense, a linebacker on defense.) I was running like a puppet whose puppeteer is in a pissy mood: jerk and jump, jerk and jump. One of the coaches, I think it was Kelly, caught sight of me and, rather than deriding me or doing a bit of imitative improv, simply screamed: "Son, run through your pads. Run through them!"

Run through your pads? What the hell was he talking about? What did the coach mean? I was used to being abused on the football field, not instructed. But this line sounded different: It sounded like someone was trying to help. Still, I had no clue what he meant.

Until suddenly and for no particular reason, grinding hard down that cement-like practice field, I did. I got it. I threw my muscles against my pads and made them part of me. You might say I accepted them rather than struggling against them. I swung my arms harder and kicked my legs forward—into my pads, through them—and suddenly I was passing guys. I was steaming ahead of a few of my fellow linemen. *Run through your pads, son!*

You had to power into the damned things. You had to apply

your muscle force against them, throw yourself through them. You had to stop believing that they were lumps of injustice. And when you did that—it took me a while to learn the lesson fully but I did—they became you and you became them and everything got better.

For once, half-decent advice wasn't lost on me. I ran through my pads and I blocked through them and I fired out my forearm shiver and from that point on, there wasn't doubt. I was going to get to the end of double sessions and I was going to be part of the team. From that day, I no longer sucked at football. I wasn't any good; I wasn't even "not bad," though I would eventually attain at least that level. But no doubt about it: I no longer sucked.

That was my first victory in the game, the first step in my football education. It wasn't learning to catch a pass or throw one (forget it), and it wasn't about becoming an ace pass blocker or vying to be named Stud of the Line by Kelly. No chance. My first victory was making it through double sessions and conquering my pads: I took an enemy and made it an ally. When I mastered my pads, I knew that I would stick with football; I knew that I'd make it.

Did I stop playing my mirror game, then? No chance. If anything, I upped the frequency.

When we got our game uniforms for our dress scrimmage against Salem, I hustled home with the flashy blue jersey— number 65 that year—and the snowy white pants with the blue military stripe down the side and my helmet and my pads. I stepped into my theater and I ran the production again—this time in full dress gear. I struck my fierce linebacker pose and I stared into the mirror.

The guy there wasn't quite me—I knew that. But somewhere inside myself I began to believe that every day with every run at the seven-man sled and every block when I managed to move my man, I was coming closer to being the guy in the mirror. It was a good feeling. I was earning the uniform day by day. And I was letting the uniform have its influence on me—on who I thought I was and who I might become.

Things weren't going well for me then. I'd become a crappy student; socially I was close to a wash; the first girl I liked in high school didn't like me and the next couple fell in line behind her. I was a bad bet socially and academically. I didn't look too good either.

My family was in bad shape. It wasn't much more than a year since my younger sister, Barbara Ann, had died, and my mother was still grieving fiercely for her. It was stunning that she managed to put food on the table every day and clean the house, do the laundry with all the filthy football gear, and take an interest in my brother and me when on some level what she wanted was to break down. Barbara Ann had been sick for three years, in and out of hospitals with one stroke after another. A stroke in a four-year-old child? A five-year-old? Six? The doctors at Massachusetts General—best hospital in the world, we were told—couldn't explain it. Barbara Ann came home from the hospital after each stroke more impaired in her speech and movement. Then she'd gain ground, slowly, slowly—with my mother taking her through exercises that, given my sister's condition, made our blocking drills and sled pushing seem easy. This went on for three years, and then she had a massive stroke and she died.

The last time I visited her in the hospital, Barbara was sitting up in a crib that looked like a steel cage. She was staring in my direction, but whether she was seeing me or not, I cannot say. Her legs were dangling outside the bars and her right hand was gripping on hard to hold her up. By that time, just before the final stroke, she could not use her left. She could no longer walk even with her usual limp. She could not talk to me; aside from a few rudimentary sounds; she had never been able to express herself at all. She was six years old at the time but she looked no more than four. She stared at me with shockingly frightened eyes, as though she were asking me, her older brother, to get her out of the horrifying cage and bring her home and make her healthy again.

On some strange level, I believed that I might be able to do this, or something like it. I came to think that if I lived a life of perfect probity and resolve she might be spared and even restored. I needed to do my homework, obey my parents, go to church, speak respectfully to all, and bear whatever slings and arrows came my way with a Christlike modesty. If I did these things, my sister would improve. She might even be healed. But I could not do them. I had become a poor student, couldn't bear school or church, disliked my teachers, and looked at my priests with deep skepticism (they all drank; a few gambled—we all knew, or we thought we did). I had made a deal with Fate, which no doubt would come through and save my sister if I fulfilled my part to the letter. But I could not keep up my end of the agreement.

When my mother and I left the hospital for the last time, she told me that she thought my sister might not be coming home. Not in a week or a month? I asked. No, she told me, not ever. Then she began to cry. Trying to sound old and paternally wise, I told my mother that it was perhaps better that way. She cried harder then. She was clearly as close to rage as she, a reasonably gentle soul, was capable of being. I tried to take it back, but how could I? You can cancel the page of a book; you can erase a blackboard; but what has been said cannot be unsaid.

My father responded to my sister's death by drinking and drinking more—and also by doing his best to show up at his job, not unduly aggravate his boss, and keep us eating digestible food and sleeping under a roof. We still watched football together sometimes. But on most Sunday afternoons he was out or working at a second job, or he was recovering from working and drinking double-time through the week. He slumped in his king-dad chair, asleep. My brother, five years younger, was a brilliant kid and did well at school and got himself some friends and had a knack for rolling with it when our parents hollered at each other. It wasn't a good scene. But everybody was *trying*. Everybody was really *trying*.

I was a high school semi-wreck. I had no car and somehow

couldn't contrive to get my license. I had about ten part-time jobs in high school, but the most representative was the one I had washing pots in the kitchen of the local hospital. When I got there in the afternoon and stepped to my station, I was hidden by dull steel basins loaded with remnants of the undigestible glop they served the patients. I was doing this to raise money to go to a formal dance with a girl who didn't want to go to the dance with me.

I was a miserable student too. I found the classes boring and I found the teachers dull. The classes were mostly boring; the teachers were frequently dull. But I was unable to see that by putting up with a few doses of tedium, I could enhance my prospects for the future no end. I had no sense of the future, or almost none. When I started playing football, the miseries of my present so absorbed me that I had no power to see past them to something else. My teachers and my guidance counselors told me I had promise: I tested well; there were some subjects I could get Bs in (history, English) without doing any work. One of my few sources of academic satisfaction in high school was being able to disappoint the people who had hopes for me. That I was radically harming my own prospects didn't much matter to me at the time.

But standing in the bathroom, lights on full force, white socks soft on the tile floor, I was different. I was one guy. I was a Medford High School football player, one of the Mustangs. And Kelly perpetually asserted that every guy on the field, from the most to the least, was part of the band, a brother to the rest.

Once I showed the seniors that I would make an effort even if I sometimes ended up back-shelled like a turtle on the ground, they accepted me. My fellow juniors did too. In the mirror all of my identity got pulled together, my self-castigating side clammed up, and my hopes to achieve something came half-alive.

When I was on the football field I was one person (or close), but outside football, life began getting a little better too. I wasn't the floundering kid that I had been. I wasn't the guy who kept saying things in class and outside and wondering: Where in the hell did *that* come from? My spirit wasn't a town meeting that had run riot; when I was in a good mood I wasn't a nice bunch of guys. And I wasn't what I had been when I'd been fighting the epic battle with my uniform and pads: a pissed-off, confused guy, squatting in the basement of himself, on strike against life. On the football field—"Run *through* your pads, son"—I was almost whole.

I was going to work and struggle until moment to moment, day to day, I was that fierce-looking fella in the glass (in his socks). Football was going to educate me into becoming myself.

Who was that guy in the mirror? He was a guy with a strong will and clear desires—shed your man; deck the ballcarrier. He was alert and ready to move. He was also well defended: He was wearing all that armor, after all. No one was going to get to him easily. He wasn't going to be knocked on his ass by anything less than a killer blow. He was poised for the next chance and he was ambitious. That guy was maybe going to pick out something to do in life and the chances were that he was going to succeed doing it—provided you thought of success in a certain way. He'd been through double sessions, after all; he'd earned the uniform.

How many other American guys have used football to develop character? Plenty, I'm sure. In America guys often grow up loved and protected, but some of them grow up too full of vanity, too pseudo-sure of themselves. But they hit sports and that changes. The coach is a tough guy and he won't pamper anyone. He bears down on all the players and holds them to one hard set of expectations. For the first time in life a guy who has been graded on a sliding scale has to meet standards. The coach only has one rule, and he applies it to everybody. As the Packers' Henry Jordan said of Vince Lombardi: "Coach treats us all the same. Treats us like dogs."

The game has a wake-up effect. You find out fast that no matter who you are, you get rewarded for hard work. It may not make you a star, but it will definitely increase your chances of starting or playing, or at least of not getting your head knocked off. If you slack on conditioning, if you don't eat right, if you drink too much, smoke too much tobacco or weed, your body will sag, your mind will go dim, and you'll get hurt. Football is God in its own way. It's uncertain whether the God above is just, but the God of football tends to be. You get out what you put in; all drops of legitimate sweat become negotiable tender.

When a boy is trying to grow up, football can be a form of education that works when no others can. The boy will listen to his coach and his teammates when he won't listen to anyone else. What he'll develop is what I began to develop on the rock-hard football practice field behind the stands at Hormel Stadium. He'll start to have an identity. He'll start to have *character*.

But what is this quality called character? What do we mean when we say that someone is in the business of acquiring it? And—a scandalous question, maybe—is character *always* a good quality to possess?

Someone with character can establish goals, laudable goals, and pursue them in an honorable way. The guy with character is focused, fixed, and steady. He makes a plan and he follows it through. When he reads a self-help book that instructs him to plan ahead, be proactive, break big tasks into smaller bits, he's comforted because that's how he does it already. When people of character fail, they pull back and reanalyze the situation. Then they draw a new game plan and hit it again. That's what Y. A. Tittle did—or so my father told me. And that's what the guy in the mirror could probably do too. "The face which character wears to me," says Ralph Waldo Emerson, "is self-sufficingness." Strange phrase (I think Emerson made it up), but that's exactly what I needed then, a dose of "self-sufficingness." During the summer that was ahead, I'd add a whole other dimension to my quest for character. But now I had a beginning.

Over time I came to understand that the objective of the game, at least for me, wasn't to score spectacular touchdowns or make bone-smashing tackles or block kicks. The game was much more about practice than about the Saturday afternoon contests. And practice was about trying to do something over and over again and failing and failing and then finally succeeding partway. Practice was about showing up and doing the same drills day after day and getting stronger and faster by tiny increments and then discovering that by the end of the season you were another person. And football was about those first days of double sessions, when everyone who stuck with it did something he imagined was impossible and so learned to recalibrate his instruments. In the future what immediately looked impossible to us— what said, Back off, not for you—had to be looked at again and maybe attempted anyway. The coaches told us this would happen; they let us know often that we were building up strength for the future, and they were right.

There were times while I was playing that I thought I was an abject failure at the game. I simply never got very good. But eventually I came to see that I was really quite a success. I was able to show up every day and work hard at something that was extremely difficult for me and to improve little by little. Football became a prototype for every endeavor in later life that required lonely, difficult work. Through the game I learned to care more about how *I* judged this or that performance of mine and less about how the world did. On the football practice field, and in mute dialogue with that guy in the mirror, I built some character for myself.

And on at least one occasion that character I created on the football field has had some direct and practical results. I badly needed it when, years later, having thrown all I thought I had into writing a chunk of my dissertation, I returned from the job market a complete flop. I had come in with hopes that pointed to the heights: I didn't want merely any academic job, though at the time that would have been hard enough. I wanted one of the dozen or so best ones that every year had about four hundred applicants apiece. If I couldn't get one, I decided, I'd quit and do something else. After the belly flop, I knew that I'd have to work on a level higher by far than anything I'd approached. I'd coasted at my ease through grad school, or so it now seemed.

I began living in the library, much the way that I lived at the football stadium my first summer on the team, arriving in the stacks early, leaving only to go to the gym in the late afternoon and to eat dinner, then returning until past dark. I built a wall of books on my table, as though to cloister myself like a medieval monk.

Did I call on the old spirit of double sessions? Quietly, pretty quietly, I did. I kept it to myself since most scholars don't see much symmetry between what they do and what runners and jumpers and (especially) blockers and tacklers attempt. I read every book in the library on John Keats, the subject of my first chapter, and most of the articles. I wrote and rewrote my first paragraph about thirty times—over and over and over again. When the summer was through I had a chapter I could be proud of and that I knew would take me where I wanted to go.

Doctoral dissertations are tougher than one might imagine. It's lonely work and no one (sometimes least of all your director, who has other things to do) cares much if you flourish or pucker on the vine. But compared to what others are compelled to endure—severe illness, divorce, the deadly sickness of a child—

sitting in an air-conditioned library and trying to make sense out of the way other people have tried to make sense of the world isn't terribly daunting. Others, I know, have called on their experience in football to summon larger doses of resolve. They've used their old sports achievements to awaken strength they had forgotten they possessed. "Diversity of strength will attend us," the poet says, "if but once we have been strong." For many of us, the time of being strong was the time when we played ball. Does football build character? Of course it does. Who could doubt it?

But character has its limits. Spend some time listening to athletes talk. I mean the good guys, the responsible guys—what are called the high-character guys. It's not only that they can be ferociously boring. They often are. But over time it becomes apparent that most have no capacity for real thought. They have no power to consider whether what they value—success, money, making the all-star team—is truly valuable. If you asked them to tell a story about their religion or their nation that departed from the rankest commonplaces, they couldn't do it. And they are about a million miles away from the higher provinces of thought where you ask yourself questions that no one has ever really resolved. What is love? What is justice? What is the Good? Listen to athletes talk. It's often about as satisfying as it would be to watch professors of philosophy play football.

Having a flexible mind is sometimes a disadvantage in sports. You've got to play by the rules, do what the coach says. You can improvise—but not too much. And an athlete will be ruined by excessive self-consciousness. Too much thinking can make you doubt your projects, doubt all the proactive and plan-ahead business. What we call character and what we should think of as real thought aren't always on good terms with each other. Athletes aren't non-thinkers because they're dumb. Some are, some aren't. They're non-thinkers chiefly because their careers reward simplicity, discipline, and conformity.

Imagination is a problem for character making too. Character building often means suppressing what's strange and maybe original about yourself. In order to unify yourself—to become that manly image in the glass—you've probably got to banish what challenges your inner balance. People with strong character pursue goals effectively. Fine. But what do they miss on the way? How many possibilities and pleasures do they skip on the road to success—or what they perceive as success?

Carl Jung said once that if people meditated enough they could completely close off access to their unconscious minds and reach full composure. The same could be said of plenty of other kinds of character-building exercises: martial arts, military drills, ballet, dressage. You can gain from those activities, but Jung's implication is right: You often lose something too.

I'm grateful for the character football helped me to build. I've needed it to progress in my profession, to publish my books and take care of my family. But my football-based character has probably come at a cost. Maybe I stanched the most imaginative and life-loving parts of myself by embracing character and identity as much as I did back there in high school staring into that mirror. I was a high school semi-loser, sure. But I was a dreamy boy, a thoughtful one, and not a dunce. I wonder what would have happened if I'd said no to character and identity and climbing the ladder and the rest. Suppose I'd chucked the uniform and gone home and picked up a book?

Samuel Taylor Coleridge, a man who in time became one of my favorite poets, wasn't long on character. Sometimes he used to look at his friend the nature poet William Wordsworth and half-swoon. Wordsworth was a man of character. Wordsworth, Coleridge liked to say, was all man! Wordsworth could do one thing at a time—and that was a major reason he was so successful. Coleridge was always moving in thirty directions at once. He spilled ink on his shirt; he wore his dressing gown all day; he was jacked on opium. You never knew what he was going to say next and neither did he, though you did know he'd say plenty and some of it would be wonderful. But Coleridge wrote "Kubla Khan" and "The Rime of the Ancient Mariner," and he wrote "Frost at Midnight," about his baby boy Hartley, maybe the loveliest poem ever written by a father to his child. Wordsworth—all man, poet of character—is a wonderful writer, but almost everything he knew he learned from the wayward, lovable Coleridge, who spent his adult life thinking that he was a failure. Did STC (as he liked to be called) have character? Not really. Not in the standard terms, not in American football terms.

But Coleridge wrote "Kubla Khan," that dreamy, magnificent, visionary poem—which he could not finish.

I don't regret my choice, not really. Without football and those grass drills and the uniform and character I might have ended up on the Bowery or one of its 1970s variants. There were plenty of those: Communes became crash pads became shooting galleries and crack houses. But as Robert Frost's speaker says in "Mending Wall": Before I built a wall I'd want to know what I was walling in and what I was walling out. Character is about wall building. It can grant security, autonomy, a stable life. But it imprisons you too. What we call character can be the enemy of imagination, empathy, invention, and of plain, pleasant dreaminess. Character preserves, but it also limits and depletes; often it does both at the same time. The coaches may not tell you so, but it's true.

2

GOING HEAD-ON: COURAGE

Midway through my first season playing ball, Tommy Lyons, the Brain, got a red skull-and-crossbones decal to wear on the side of his helmet. The coaches presented it to him in honor of his ferocious play. He and Paul Brentano were the only ones to earn skull-and-bones stickers that year. Paul was a radically undersized linebacker. He must have weighed about 140 pounds, but like Tommy he was a fierce tackler. One hit of his canceled the afternoon for the star fullback from Everett. I was close by on the sidelines when Paul delivered it, and you could feel shock waves. Paul and Tommy were the two guys on the team that the coaches called "real football players."

Weren't the rest of us real football players? Yes and no. We'd earned the uniforms and that was something. But according to the Mustang coaches, football players were hitters. They were guys who loved to get into demolition-derby mode and wreck the opposition—and didn't mind wrecking themselves too, if need be. By the time they got their skulls and crossbones, Tommy and Paul were regularly coming out of the locker room mummied up in tape. Tommy walked with a limp; Paul sometimes staggered from place to place. But when it was time to step into the game, they enjoyed miracle transformations.

The quarterbacks and the running backs and the ends didn't set the tone for our team. They weren't at the highest-level, football players. They didn't live to smash other guys. Insofar as we had a group identity, Tommy and Paul were at the heart of it. We'd win games—we'd win every game, the coaches told us—if we all made ourselves over in their image.

We had a ritual to consolidate our fierce sense of team identity. After running up and down a sharp bank several thousand times (or so it seemed), we came together in a clump. Then, when we were woozy with fatigue from the Pit and giddy with relief to have the running behind us, the captains led us in what was called a "war cry." "Be rough!" the left side of the clump screamed, echoing one captain in a call and response. "Be tough!" the right side bellowed, echoing the other captain. Then all at once, young lungs breaking out together with the sound: "Be a football player!" Even flat-out tired and grateful for the respite, some of us half-smiled at the kindergarten simplicity. But there it was—that's what we aspired to as a group. Be rough and be tough. Be a football player!

Was it beside the point to slap a dime store decal on Tommy's and Paul's hats and to get us crying out about being rough and tough? Not a bit. The coaches knew what the game was about.

The game was about violence. It was about creating a mentality that would allow—maybe it would even compel—young guys to do something that is, to say the least, counterintuitive. We had to throw our bodies in the direction of other, oncoming human bodies and do it with as much force as we could. Most people do not want to do that. It makes no immediate sense to turn into a missile and launch into space at another object. You may not get up again. Or worse (to some sensibilities), he may not. Just so, almost no one *readily* wants to step onto a battlefield and bayonet the guy racing toward him in a uniform only a bit differently hued and designed than his own.

At the center of our education through football was having a capacity for violence instilled in us—or coaxed out of us. Guys who clearly didn't "like to hit" were always looked at askance, even though some of them were our most valuable skill players. They were called on constantly to deliver blows in practice and to absorb them so as to prove that even if they did have their reservations about contact, they were still part of the team. This game was about violence—hit and be hit. We had to affirm that over and over again, and we had to do it together. Ready on the right! (Ready.) Ready on the left! (Ready.) Well then . . .

In the first weeks of practice I had learned something about character. I'd begun to pull myself together. I'd earned the uniform, and I was proud of it. And the uniform was now an ally. Looking at myself in the mirror padded and helmeted, I got an inkling of the sort of person I wanted to be and maybe was becoming. (Though all of that may have been happening at a cost.) But there was a second step in my football education, and that was going to prove more difficult to negotiate. To really be a football player, I was going to have to learn something about courage.

During most of my first year playing, I wasn't a candidate for a skull-and-crossbones decal, not even close. Often I was scared. When we lined up for one-on-one drills I strained to see where Tommy the Brain and Victor Guest, the guy he vied with for Stud, were in line and put myself where I wouldn't have to face them. (Paul was a terror in games, but he was hurt so often that he frequently missed practice or went half-speed.) One-on-one was blocker versus tackler with a running back behind the blocker. The idea was for the blocker to clear away the defensive man and let the runner break through. When I saw Tommy three guys away from the front of the line and myself three back on my side, my body trembled, and on more than one occasion I contrived to drop down a few spaces to miss the pain—and the embarrassment, which I feared almost as much. Once during the first weeks, I actually tried to tackle the Brain, who played tight end on offense, and I ended up on the ground, clutching on to his ankle. He didn't seem to think it worthwhile to shake me off.

I was part of the team. I'd earned my jersey by showing up every day for double-session practices and doing all the conditioning drills and never missing a session and always giving 100 percent effort and the rest. But I was supposed to be a lineman— a hitter, a banger—and instead I was scared. Guys smaller than I was would lead with their heads when they blocked and tackled. They made resoundingly violent pops. (The ferocious Paul Brentano was *way* smaller than I was.) But I didn't have the guts for it.

I upbraided myself constantly. Lying in bed at night, I imagined myself going at the game the right way. I pictured the star fullback, Phil McNamara, coming at me and watched as I lowered my shoulders, bulled my neck, and shot forward, my helmet going square into his gut. He fell like he'd been hit by something from a catapult. The next afternoon, there was Phil, ball in hand, and there was I, with legs bowed and shoulders pitched slightly forward (my form was actually pretty good), but when the moment came, I didn't lead with my head or even with my shoulder. I veered off, or dove and went for his ankles. The coaches took it in and shared looks of manly exasperation.

Every day I went out onto the practice field resolved to be brave, and every day I had my script for how I was going to do it. And every day I failed. At night I'd berate myself, run the movies of myself blocking and tackling the right way, and resolve to show up and do what I was supposed to do. But I couldn't. I was scared. I was like a kid who couldn't dive headfirst into the water. (I wasn't crazy about doing that either.) When the moment of truth came, I chickened out. There was a TV show that had been on a few years before called *Branded*, about a young man in the U.S. Cavalry who'd been accused of cowardice and thrown out of the army in disgrace. Sometimes I'd hear the theme song in my head—once you heard it you didn't forget it, or the lyrics either. "All but one man died there at Bitter Creek / And they said he ran away!" But that kid was innocent; he was actually no coward at all.

I had company in my sorry state. A number of my fellow linemen weren't really in love with head banging, either. They tended to be large, soft-bodied guys whose dads desperately wanted them to play, but who would have preferred to be at home in the afternoon, munching sandwiches and watching TV. Their fathers showed up at practice (didn't they have jobs?), stood on the sidelines, and winced along with the coaches as their sons drew themselves into protective crouches when they should have been creating mayhem. The dads watched the one-on-one drills and as their kids flopped, the dads stomped the ground or cursed or flipped their cigarettes away in disgust.

The one-on-one drill was the equivalent of single combat. It smacked of the duel and of the man-to-man encounters, fights to the death, that punctuate great epic poems, like *The Iliad*. Paris, who has stolen Helen away from Greece, takes on her lawful husband, Menelaus; Hector, prince of the Trojans, fights with Ajax, an oxlike muscleman. Then at the close of the poem Hector faces off with Achilles, the most fearsome of the Greeks, son of the mortal Peleus and the sea nymph Thetis. Hector has killed Achilles's dear friend Patroclus, and now Achilles is in a rage. He carves up the Trojan troops and finally he encounters Hector alone outside the walls of the city. All of the Greeks are massed on the plain to watch the encounter. The Trojans, men and women and children, stand along the walls of Troy to see their champion go against the best of the Greeks. Hector's parents, Priam, the lord of the city, and his wife, Hecuba, gaze down from the walls to watch the fight.

A one-on-one football drill, on a scrub field behind Hormel Stadium or even on a manicured, lavishly irrigated lawn in Green Bay, Wisconsin, or Foxborough, Massachusetts, is a pale shadow of this kind of epic encounter. The player who falls to the ground in defeat and temporary disgrace will roll over, jump to his feet, and brush himself off. He'll head to the back of the line and give it one more try. For the losing warrior in single combat, this usually won't be the case. Though, to be sure, no one dies in the duel between Menelaus and Paris, or even the one between Hector and Ajax. It's all about standing.

Every game resembles war. Tennis, soccer, lacrosse: You might say that they all domesticate violence. (Even Ping-Pong has some displaced violence in it, especially if you go at it full-throttle the way the Olympic players do.) Boxing isn't a subli-mation of war—it is war. One man tries to destroy another; that's the central aim. You play football and baseball and basket-ball, Joyce Carol Oates says. But no one "plays" boxing. All sports may be built on war, but some are nearer to it than others. Of the games I know, football comes closest to war without falling over the border and becoming war pure and simple. George Carlin captures this in his famous bit about football and baseball: "In football the object is for the quarterback, also known as the field general, to be on target with his aerial assault, riddling the de-fense by hitting his receivers with deadly accuracy in spite of the blitz. With short bullet passes and long bombs he marches his troops into enemy territory, balancing the aerial assault with a sustained ground attack that punches holes in the wall of the enemy's defensive line."

There you have it. The language of football is the language of warfare—and Carlin doesn't mention the sack, the trenches, and a few other verbal mergers. There's also the warlike mind-set that goes with the game: Victory is all! Carlin doesn't quote what's probably the most famous line about football, though it would have fit into his spiel fine. It comes from Vince Lombardi: "Winning isn't everything, it's the only thing." You've got to beat the opponent by outscoring him, sure, but you also want to thrash him physically—not just beat him, but beat him up. Be a football player! Dominate him! Win!

The essential quality that a football player needs is identical to the warrior's essential virtue. Both need to be brave. Both need to possess courage. But of course, there is courage and there is *courage*. Back at its origins, the Western tradition gives us two very different versions of what courage is, what it means, and where it comes from. Those versions, not surprisingly, come out of *The Iliad*.

One model of ideal courage is Hector. Hector is a prince of the Trojans, the most valiant son of Priam and Hecuba. He's a ferocious warrior. He's always in the forefront, leading the Trojans and their allies against the Greeks, who have come to reclaim Helen. Hector inspires fear in his enemies, and affection and trust in his fellow Trojans. They will follow him anywhere because he's strong and brave and shirks no danger. He faces off man-to-man against the terrifying Greek giant Ajax, and while he does not overthrow Ajax, he holds his own. During his greatest run as a warrior, he leads the Trojans down to the beach and the Greek camp, and almost succeeds in burning their ships. At the climax of his triumphal episode, Hector (with the help of another Trojan warrior and a god) manages to kill Patroclus, the dear friend of the Greeks' mightiest fighter, Achilles.

But Hector isn't simply a warrior. He can also be a remarkably gentle, thoughtful man. Only two of the Trojans, we learn, treat Helen, whom Paris has stolen from her Greek husband, Menelaus, and brought to Troy, with any kindness. Most see her as a whore and the cause of the war to boot. But Priam and Hector behave with humanity to her; they see that the situation isn't her fault. Wisely, they owe the war to Fate and to the gods. Hector is also an admirable husband and father. In one of the most moving scenes in the poem, we see him coming in from the battlefield covered with grime and blood. He marches into his living quarters and meets his wife, Andromache, and her maid, holding their baby, Astyanax, the boy the Trojans call "the prince of the city."

When Astyanax sees the horrifying armored man smashing his way toward him and then reaching out to hold him, he bursts into frightened tears. Hector understands immediately. He pulls off his blazing bronze helmet with its horsehair plume and he lays it down gently on the floor. His son sees who it is and laughs with joy. My father! Hector takes the boy in his arms and dandles him with all the tenderness of a mother.

Homer suggests something important about Hector in the scene: Hector is two men. He is the warrior who fights ferociously on the plains of Troy and who can stand against the terrifying Ajax. But he can shift into another identity. He can become gentle, courtly, nearly sweet natured. We see this side of him when he talks with his wife, Andromache. They are clearly not only husband and wife but also true friends. No two people in the poem talk together at the level of ready intimacy that they do. When they are talking that day in the halls, Hector says something quite revealing about himself. He is describing his life as a warrior and how he came to be where he is, and at a certain point he says: I have *learned* how to step into the middle of the fray and deal death to my enemies.

I have *learned*. (As the scholar David Mikics observes, the Greek word is *didaskein* and it occurs only this once in the poem.) Homer's point is subtle, but it is there. Hector is not a natural warrior. He had to learn to do what he does on the battlefield. He is not by nature fierce or proficient with weapons. He *can be* both of those things, but they're not really at the core of his being. Hector was probably born to be a statesman. During the poem he seems to be something like his father's prime minister, and it is clear that he would go on to be a superb king of Troy sometime in the future—if Troy had a future, which it does not.

Hector is the warrior that many humane, thoughtful individuals would like to be, assuming that they had to go into battle at all. To put it crudely, Hector can turn it off. When the war isn't burning, when the battle is over, he goes back to being dignified, thoughtful, and considerate of other human beings. His first and most essential self is manifest then, the self that smiles at Astyanax and unfolds his secret fears and his hopes to his wife. Hector is the prototype for the soldier who is fierce in war but who would never hurt a noncombatant and never torture a prisoner. When the war is over, this kind of fighter will return contentedly to civilian life, put his medals in a velvet case, and store them in the attic. His modesty will be with him all the time.

The athlete who has Hector-like courage never throws a low blow, never cheats, treats his adversaries with respect, and always remembers "it's just a game." There are pursuits in his life that matter more to him than scoring touchdowns. He is courtly, reserved, and decent. On the field, he goes all out. He competes from the beginning of the game to the end and he wants to win. But like Hector, he has his pride in being human and humane. Like Hector, he can turn it off.

There is one problem with being Hector: Hector loses. Not only does he lose; he is humiliated and degraded. For eventually Hector must face Achilles, and Achilles is a different order of being. Achilles does not have two identities the way Hector does. He is not a man of war and a man of peace. Achilles is a pure warrior, and on the day he learns that Hector has killed Patroclus, he goes nearly mad with fury. He rampages up and down the field, looking for Hector. But before he finds him, Achilles creates massive destruction. He kills one wave of Trojans after another and he does it without mercy.

A young Trojan he has overthrown grasps Achilles by the knees and begs for his life. Achilles laughs. Look at me, he says: so large, so beautiful, so strong and swift. Someday I too will die. But this is not my day. It is yours. Achilles murders so many Trojans that their bodies glut the river Scamander, which becomes enraged, leaps its banks, and chases him across the plains, eager to drown him.

Achilles is from a different order than Hector, and not only because he is the son of a goddess. Achilles is purely a warrior: He has no other, more humane identity. He lives for one thing and that is to be the best of the Greeks, the most ferocious and deadly of their warriors, and he is. He is amazingly strong, adept with all weapons, and inhumanly fast. If you stand your ground, he'll overpower you; if you retreat, he'll run you down. Achilles wants glory more than anything else. Hector lives to defend his city and his people, and to nurture his family. Achilles lives to set the standard for warriors for all time. He aspires to be what Shakespeare's Cleopatra called her beloved Antony: "the soldier's pole," the man by whom other warriors will be measured.

When Achilles and Hector meet outside the walls of Troy, with both armies looking on, there is no real contest. But it is not only that Hector loses and is bound to lose. Hector runs. He races around the walls of Troy time after time, until finally he's prevailed on to stop and to fight. He looks foolish; he looks like a coward (which he never has been) before the fierce, unified force that is Achilles. When they finally face each other, Hector the humane warrior asks for terms. He wants to talk about how the victor might return the body of the vanquished; he wants to talk about mourning and burial rites. Achilles won't hear any of it. He tells Hector that he is in such a rage that when Hector dies he may eat his flesh raw. In a few minutes Hector is dead. With his dying breath, he tells Achilles that soon he too will be gone—to which the greatest of the Greeks tells him in sum that he doesn't give a damn. Achilles knows that he will be remembered as he wishes to be and so whether he dies now or lives another day is a matter of near indifference.

In the last battle with Achilles, Hector is surely frightened and he shows it. But eventually he musters his courage and he stands against a superior foe and pays. As for Achilles, he simply does not seem to have much fear to contend with. He is always ready for war, always fierce, always deadly. Hector reveals another self when his helmet comes off. Achilles might be a little less frightening when he removes the golden helmet that the blacksmith god Hephaestus made for him, but not much.

Who would not like to be Hector, the great warrior who is also an admirable human being? Who would not want to have a kind of courage that one can—most of the time—summon up to save what must be saved? But of course there's a problem with Hector's sort of courage. Hector loses.

As for me with the Medford Mustangs, marinating in my cowardice, I barely knew who Hector and Achilles were, and probably would not have known how to draw useful lessons from them even if I had managed to read Homer's book. I had my own resources to figure this matter out, and my resources, though still meager, had been growing. I could think about the problem, or begin to. My training in character helped me to do that. It helped me to isolate my difficulty and set objectives. And in time I did arrive at something like a solution. The solution, though, came at a cost.

One day we were in the clubhouse watching films of our recent game. Somehow I'd been summoned off the bench and into the game at linebacker. I hadn't been in there long, but I'd still managed to make a terrible mistake. On a pass play, I'd given up my assignment to drop back into coverage and I'd gone after the quarterback, because one of my dopey teammates, a senior, told me to. I blitzed and got tangled in the middle of the line, and their tight end snatched a pass in my zone. Touchdown. The coaches ran the film once and then they ran it again. "Who is that?" Kelly hollered. "Who is that linebacker?" He darn well knew, I'm sure. But he asked anyway. No one said anything, least of all me. He ran the play backward and I had the pleasure of seeing myself in awkward jerks and stutters doing what I'd done wrong in reverse. "Is that you, Edmundson?" I admitted that it was. Then from Kelly, the crucial line: "You ain't *never* gonna play."

I felt like I'd been jabbed in the solar plexus, harder than I'd ever been hit on the football field. The air went out of me, and I couldn't take any in. "You ain't never gonna play!" Never! Never? No matter what I did? No matter how hard I worked? I was never going to play. I was never going to get into a game again. That sentence boomed around in my head with the sound of a bass drum. Never, never, never. At first when I thought of the words, as I did fifty times over the next days, I was completely smashed: I'd been humiliated. I'd been clowned in public.

But then something happened. We were scrimmaging, top offense against the defensive reserves—and I was naturally with the reserves. Almost every play they tore us up. They came up the middle and isolated the linebacker—me—so that the blocking back could clock him under the chin. Then the running back came roaring through. Or else they ran a sweep, two guards pulling, Green Bay Packers–style, and I had to slide to the strong side and try to meet the ballcarrier. No dice: I got blown over by one of those twin guards, squat and powerful as chessboard rooks. The sweeps and the isolations were the worst: but I also got burned on short passes into my zone. And on the rare chance I was assigned to rush the quarterback I ended up in a mishmash of players somewhere around the center. Did I ever tackle the quarterback? On some blitzes I didn't see him.

But the sweeps were when I was most often humiliated, and it was usually my own doing. I was so scared of the contact that I contrived to miscalculate the speed of the back. I'd cut in after him too early, and even if I managed to dodge those squat guards, I'd miss him from behind. Or I'd mess it up the other way. I'd take an angle that put me so far in front of the runner that he would already have galloped thirty yards before I arrived and by then the whistle would have blown.

I was ducking the hits. A tackle on a sweep is often a high-impact affair. If you're going to bring the guy down, you really have to slam him, wrap him up, and throw him onto the ground. I wanted none of this kind of action. It was too brutal. It was too dangerous.

I had become expert in pantomiming my frustration when once again I'd messed up and taken the wrong angle to the ball-carrier. I threw my arms down at my sides; I gazed at the heavens; I expelled a pillar of air through my fragile white face mask.

Then one day, after I'd been run by and run through a few times, that nasty line of the coach's soared through my head, like an ugly birdsong. "You ain't never gonna play." And again and again. "Never, you ain't never gonna play." And rather than simply humiliating me, the line made me mad. Who was he or anyone else to tell me that I was going to fail forever? I was a steaming failure now, OK—so I was. But no one has a magic glass; no one has a bubbling cauldron to look into and see the future. Ain't never gonna play! Really? Really!

I said it to myself again and again. And the next play they ran a sweep. They ran it to my left—the direction I moved best. And this time rather than conspiring with myself to miscalculate the point of contact and do my little dance of manly frustration after I did, I took a bead on the back and moved for him. He was a big kid and fast and he had a good head of steam going. I took long proud steps toward him and somehow dodged the blockers who surrounded my man like bodyguards moving the king through a crowd.

The back never saw me coming. I was a half step behind him and outside his peripheral vision and I slammed him. He did not squirm and he did not fight; he went over onto the ground in an instant. Bang.

And it didn't hurt me at all! It turned out that when you delivered the blow it didn't cause pain, or at least not pain you felt right then. That was a secret worth knowing, wasn't it? I was afraid of the game—but being afraid and holding back, I was already taking the hardest hits that football offered. The tackling dummy takes the most brutal thwacks and never hurts anyone back, doesn't it?

Man, was that runner surprised when he staggered up to see who had planted him. And the coaches saw it too. "Darn," said Kelly. "That is the way to tackle."

I used my mantra in one-on-one drills too. Sometime around the day of the flying tackle (maybe before, maybe after) I got in line against a capable guard and an Ajax-like ox of a kid. I said my magic words to myself. "Never, never, never." Ajax was carrying the ball; the other guy was blocking—or he was going to try to.

"You ain't never gonna play," I said to myself. "Never." And as I said it, the rage rose like red tide. I popped the blocker so hard that he fell to the ground like a rag doll and when the ballcarrier saw me heading for him he cringed. I put my helmet smack into his gut and down went Ajax like a bag of wet cement.

Well, I'd figured it out, hadn't I? I could push myself into something like a rage by whispering the right words. I had an incantation that turned me from one guy into another. (What more magic can a human being command?) The spell didn't make me any faster or quicker or more athletic, but it did make me something like brave. With it, I could stick my head in. With it I could pitch myself into blocking and tackling, the way the tough guys did. Other players saw it and they began to avoid me in drills. The coaches saw it too, and though they weren't disposed to throw me into the games much more, they began to treat me in a different way.

What had I done? What exactly was the magic that I had worked? The phrase—"you ain't never gonna play"—was something like a match, a stick with a sulfur tip. It was hot in itself, and I could also use it to ignite my shame and my resentment and my anger at the world. My spirit was full of such stuff—rancor and rage—which had come from all my boyhood defeats. There were the times I'd been teased for being too fat or four-eyed; the times I'd been almost the last picked and then laughed at for it; the times that a girl I had liked failed to acknowledge my existence—there was no end to the list. It was like I had a basement full of old, yellowed newspapers tied up in bundles, and paint-stained cloths and jars of turpentine and oil. When you applied a match, it lit up.

I became pretty good at applying the match—or rather matches, because there was more than one way to get the fire going. And I also found that certain cues to anger would get used up. "You ain't never gonna play" became old hat in time. Hearing it internally only made me irritated when what I wanted was something close to rage. So I became a collector of resentments. I created a personal dictionary of insults that had been visited on me. Of these one stood out—it touched the limits.

The day that my sister was buried, we brought her coffin up to the front door of the church for her funeral mass. Somehow there materialized between her coffin and the door a group of kids playing with a colorful rubber kick ball. For what seemed like five minutes, though it could not have been more than one or two, nothing anyone did could get them out of the way. One kid in particular wouldn't budge. He was small and a touch frail and he wore oversize rubber boots, sloppily buckled. Even after the rest of the group dispersed, he stood before the coffin, fussing with the ball, rolling it and kicking it and stumbling over it. It was all I could do not to go after that little kid—who could not have been more than seven and was probably younger—and pluck him up like a weed from the ground and throw him aside in a heap.

Then and afterward I hated the kid with a blood hate that surpassed articulation. And when I wanted true rage, it was to his image that I turned. There he was in my mind's eye, noodling with the ball in his innocent, stupid way in front of my sister's coffin. And I was in a fury. By thinking of this I was activating emotions of so powerful and primary a nature that I should rightly have been terrified of them. I was connecting with the human rage against death and with the primal furor that can come when you realize that when you lose someone you love that person will not be coming back, not ever. And that life will go on and that no one—truly—who is not directly connected really much cares about it at all.

I used anything I needed to inflame myself and then I went full tilt. I rammed my head into anyone who moved toward me and was on the other squad. But was that courage? Was I really being brave when I called on those images and those words?

Even the great Achilles suffers humiliation. *The Iliad* begins when the king of the Greek armies, Agamemnon, humbles Achilles in front of all the troops. He takes away Achilles's woman, Briseis, when the king is compelled to return his own prize, Chryseis, to her father. Achilles insists that Briseis was more than a concubine to him. "I loved Briseis," he cries out. Achilles could easily murder Agamemnon on the spot. The king couldn't stand for a moment against the warrior in his rage. But the gods won't permit Achilles to do the deed. Athena grabs his sword hand before he can act. Father Zeus, monarch of heaven and earth, is not well disposed to the killing of kings.

So the hero has to retire to his tent in rage and shame. He sits there fuming, nursing his grudges and building anger. Anger is what the poem is all about. *The Iliad* begins with the words "Anger be now your song, immortal one"—by immortal one, Homer means the muse, which he invokes to help him sing of rage that is "doomed and ruinous." He doesn't say, "Courage be now your song"—it's anger.

Before the end of the poem, Achilles is humiliated again. In a crisis he sends his dear friend Patroclus out to fight in his stead. Achilles lends Patroclus his armor and tells him to throw the Trojans back, but only so far. Patroclus is hungry for glory himself, though. (Maybe he's tired of being under Achilles's thumb. Maybe he too is suffering humiliation.) He pushes the Trojans back and back some more. He goes too far. And then he meets Hector, and with the help of a god and another Trojan, Hector cuts Patroclus down.

Again Achilles is humiliated. Why didn't he go out himself into the wars? Why did he send his dearest friend? It is rage, yes, but it is also, I think, humiliation at his selfishness that sends Achilles flaming into the battle where he will eventually fight and kill Hector. Is Achilles brave? His bravery, if it is that, comes in part from a hunger to redeem his humiliations and restore his lost manhood. His courage comes (as mine did, as the courage of many others may as well) at least partially from humiliation. His drive to compensate for his shame brings him close to being a beast. I'm so enraged I could eat your flesh, he tells Hector. That is the way of the lion and the wolf but not the way of a man.

Football players and soldiers constantly behave like Achilles. They go berserk. Whether they are fed by shame or primal rage or some other more noble quality, it is not easy to say. But we can say this: Those who have access to their rage often triumph. The linebacker Lawrence Taylor changed the game of football with his speed and ferocity. No quarterback was safe from his furious blitzes. Offensive line play had to be reconceived to deal with Taylor and those who imitated his style. By his own admission

Taylor turned himself into something like an animal. He was an assassin on the field. Off the field he was all about cocaine and fast driving and sex with whoever. (Taylor says that he once showed up at a Giants team meeting in handcuffs, after spending a night with a pair of call girls.) His coach, Bill Parcells, knew about this behavior (more or less) and turned a blind eye to it because he felt it fed Taylor's on-field fire. Taylor, I suppose, was another avatar of Achilles in his wrath. Against him, Hector often hasn't much of a chance.

My father's idol, Jim Brown, seemed to embody the role of Hector. Brown played his nine seasons, averaged his more than five yards a carry, and dominated almost every game he entered. At times Jim Brown simply *was* the Cleveland Browns. And he was a splendidly dignified man both on the field and off. He never seemed to lose his temper, even after a dirty or late hit. (His nemesis, Sam Huff, of the Giants, appeared to specialize in both.) After a run that went for twenty yards and combined bull's strength with catlike balance, Jim Brown rose slowly and walked back to the huddle with perfect composure. Competitive intensity? He could turn it on and off, or so it seemed. These qualities made my father love Jim Brown and made him offer Brown to me as a paragon of men.

But after Jim Brown left football another side of him either developed or became visible. He was in trouble with the law and was brought up on domestic violence charges; he did jail time for smashing the window of his wife's car. There were constant stories about Jim Brown and domestic trouble. He still could display extraordinary dignity. No other former player drew the kind of respect from young guys fresh to the game that Jim Brown did. But the later behavior suggests that all along he may have been fed as much by rage as Lawrence Taylor was. He may have been more Achilles than Hector.

Everyone wants to be Hector—in war and in sports. Everyone wants the dual identity of humane citizen and fierce warrior. But everyone wants to win as well. I wonder sometimes if Hector-like talk and bearing aren't fictions that we use to cover over our brutal and selfish drives. I wonder sometimes if there really is a kind of courage that differs from the courage of Achilles. I wonder if, in life, Hector really exists.

We might also call the kind of courage that Achilles possesses "offensive courage." It is the courage of the initiator, the guy who starts the fights. Homer's Greeks are invaders. One might even say that they are colonialists. They come from far away and though their ostensible motive is to rescue Helen, Homer makes it clear that most of them are in it for the glory and treasure. The Greeks talk constantly about all the wealth that's stashed in the citadel of Troy. Achilles, with his aggressive dispatch, has the courage of the empire builder; he fights with the rage of the man who lands in a strange country and battles for his reputation and for conquest. It is odd and very off-putting to think of American warriors in these terms now, but if you look around the globe and if you ask our adversaries, you may see that we too are invaders, or at least perceived as such. Achilles's courage is the courage of expanding empire—it is, maybe, a version of our own courage in the world now.

What about me, and my education in courage? I became more of a football player: I could run with the team and now I could hit with the team too. That was no small achievement for someone who had started out as a timid boy. I developed some guts. And there's no doubt that I became more confident off the field too. I was more likely to speak my mind, more likely to go after what I wanted. I wasn't as self-doubting as I'd been.

As I developed some physical prowess and some willingness to risk my body in a headlong tackle, I became a little more sure of myself at home too. I had always held my father in awe. I loved his quick, harsh tongue (at least when his judgments weren't directed at me), his fiery intelligence, and his rebellious attitude toward the world. I'd heard him sound off when a cop or a boss tried to push him around and I relished it. I'd come to believe that he was something like indomitable.

My mother told me a story about how he'd been jumped by four guys (sometimes it was five, occasionally six) while he was in high school. They'd come into the restaurant where he was working, and they were drunk and rude to my mother, who was sitting in a booth with her sister. My father told them to leave. They told him that this was highly unlikely. (My mother thought they might have been soldiers home from the war.) He put a hand on one and yanked him up and immediately all four (or five or six) were on him. I could picture my father in his kitchen whites struggling manfully with a bunch of drunken infantrymen for my mother's honor. "One was punching him," my mother said, "one was kicking him, and there was another who was trying to do I don't know what to him." How did it come out? I asked my mother whenever I got her to retell the story, which I did a few dozen times. "He did well," my mother said with an indulgent smile. "He more than held his own." I badgered her. He did well? How well? Did he win? My mother had a kindly soul—after five or six iterations of the tale, my father turned out to have whipped them all quite soundly.

Sharp mind, fast tongue, good with his hands, always ready to mix it up: That's who my father was to me even into my early high school years. But football made me bigger and stronger and I began to see that my father now was thin and almost frail in his limbs and chest and that his beer was catching up with him and expanding his belly. (It looked like it had been pumped up with a bicycle pump.) I sized him up now in the way football players do: not big enough, not strong enough, not the guy he thought he was. I had developed the athlete's none-too-charming habit of seeing people as their bodies and not much more. When I looked at another guy, I conducted a quick assessment. One-on-one, head-to-head: Could he take me, or could I take him?

Every guy has to come to terms with his own growth and his father's decline, and usually that coming to terms doesn't begin charitably. (Though in time the feelings for an aging parent can become surpassingly tender.) I'd had a late start in the standard process of learning that my father wasn't perfect in much of any way and that what he said about himself exceeded what he ever did or would do. (How long, I wonder, did I keep telling myself those Geronimo stories?) But the step away from the father is a necessary one, and my football education made it start to happen.

I was becoming a little more likely to disagree with my father—in my own mind and sometimes aloud. When he ran down the Kennedys, which he did often, even though Teddy was the last one alive and in politics, I could see envy and resentment, where before I'd seen only sharp-minded criticism. When a friend's father bought a brand-spanking-new car, a Ford LTD, my father dubbed it a Little Tin Dumpster. I laughed, sure, but now I could see that my father's wit (which was often better than this sally) was based in resentment and frustration as much as in any sort of accurate, independent perception. "You'd take an LTD if somebody gave it to you for free," I told my father. Meaning an LTD, whatever its flaws and however overpriced, was better than the rust bucket Cadillac, ten years old at least, bearing a three-foot sign on the roof endorsing a local politician whose record was none too clean, that my father had parked outside our house, occasionally in front of the nearest fire hydrant. "Malarkey," he said. (My father never admitted defeat.) "A Cadillac is a Cadillac."

My education in football was making me more sure of myself. But I became more brutal too. After my first football season ended, I found myself in one-on-one fistfights and a few all-in brawls. I wasn't a thug—far from it. But I drank and caroused and behaved in reckless ways that I probably never would have had I not put a uniform on and learned to bang, a man among men. And the "courage" that I generated in those fights—where did it come from? It sometimes came from replaying my humiliations. I brought them out from the corners of my spirit and I played them over again, in slow motion, until I was boiling. Is this bravery?

Even now, the imprint of the game and the "courage" that I learned there are still with me. Not long ago I surprised a friend—and myself—by telling him that if someone had the temerity to smash up my car (which I loved far too much), my responding with a punch in the mouth wouldn't be completely impossible. I recognize in myself a capacity for violence that's well beyond that of most middle-class guys in middle age, and I have to be vigilant about it. But I also recognize in myself a willingness to go my own way, say what I think, and take the inevitable hits. And this may owe at least in part to the courage I learned by whatever means (and however imperfectly) on a football field. We pay for our sins, to be sure. But even for our virtues there is sometimes a price. I think that everyone who has learned courage from football has got to recognize what it may cost, no matter what the coaches and the boosters say. Character often costs something; courage can come with a price.

3

THE SOMERVILLE GAME: LOSING

We Mustangs were winners. The coaches told us that from the first day of practice, and we believed them. When we did our grass drills—yelling and sweating and pounding our thigh pads with our palms—we yelled it out: Nine and 0! Nine and 0!

Nine wins, no losses! The Medford Mustangs had been undefeated the year before and won the Greater Boston League championship. They'd beaten Everett and Revere, two perennially tough squads, and on the last day of the season, they had beaten Malden, the team that was supposed to be Medford's major rival. The game took place on Thanksgiving Day and the stands were always full.

Nine and 0! Nine and 0! When we chanted those numbers we were looking back to the great, undefeated season. All of the seniors on the field had been part of the unbeaten year. By having earned our uniforms and been accepted by the other players, we juniors were part of the legacy too. Nine and 0! Nine and 0! Unbeaten and untied: champions of the Greater Boston League.

When we took up the chant, we were looking back to the heroic season, but we were looking ahead too. We too were going to go undefeated. We were going to be Greater Boston League champs. Before the season began we took up the Nine and 0 chant at every practice. (We saved our war cry—Be a football player!—for special days.) Before going out to practice, it wasn't uncommon for one player to look at another and say simply: "Nine and 0." We greeted each other outside of practice with the winner's mantra too. Passing a fellow ballplayer in the corridor, we might say hello or nod our heads, but we might also just say, "Nine and 0!" If it was a senior passing by a junior, it was the senior's right to deploy the phrase (or not). It would have been sacrilege for a junior to do it. But when a senior gave you the password, you were within your rights to echo it back to him. "Nine and 0." A pause, a grim smile, then the countersign, "Nine and 0." When Jack O'Brien, the center and cocaptain, passed me in the corridor one day not long after double sessions had ended and said the sacred words, I felt a happy shiver go up my back. "Nine and 0," Jack said. And I replied, as I had to: "Nine and 0."

We started the season well enough: We beat Chelsea and Watertown, two teams that were game enough but not terribly talented, and also, according to Kelly, abysmally coached. "Who is coaching this defense? Who?" Kelly muttered as we watched game films in which the Chelsea squad overloaded the wrong side of the field and got rolled over for a touchdown. I'm sure he was tempted to spit on the locker room floor to express his disdain—but if he was, the cold eye of the head coach held him back.

So now we were two and 0, two and 0. So we varied our chants. We slapped our pads and screamed defiance at our enemies and looked up into the bright New England sky of early fall. And like good Homeric warriors we bragged. We told the world about our current record—two wins and no losses—and we told the world about our record to be: nine wins, no losses, no ties. Nine and 0, baby, nine and 0!

When Alabama football fans meet, they greet each other with the sacred words "Roll Tide." Christians say, "Christ be with you," and Buddhists say, "Namaste" ("The light in me greets the light in you"). When followers of the Gallic psychoanalyst Jacques Lacan met each other on the boulevards of Paris, they purportedly asked, "Where do you stand in regard to your desires?" (I'm sure it sounds better in French.) We said: Nine and zip! We said: Nine and 0!

But now we had to play Somerville. Somerville wasn't Chelsea and it wasn't Watertown. When you asked the players who'd been on the team last year about the season, you naturally expected them to talk about the Malden game, one of the oldest high school rivalries in the country. "Piece of cake," Jack O'Brien, who'd started at center and starred at linebacker the previous year, said. "Piece of cake." "It was tit," one of the other guys said. "Nothing but tit." (How "tit" had come to be synonymous with "easy," I cannot tell you, but it had.) Malden the previous year was no problem, or not much. So what *was* tough about the season?

Somerville. What was hard about them? I wanted to know. "You'll see," the seniors said. "You wait and see."

Somerville was a tough, largely Italian city that stood between Medford and Cambridge. In time much of Somerville would become a cushy enclave, full of young professionals and well-off students from Harvard and MIT. But in 1968 it was nothing like that. Somerville was a city full of tough guys who beat each other bloody outside bars, and inside them when they felt moved. It was their major form of recreation. The town was reputed to have more barrooms and liquor stores per capita than any other in the country. People said it was as densely populated as Hong Kong. Mobsters shot each other in the street in Somerville. Cops opened the trunks of cars sitting out in factory parking lots to find one or sometimes two bodies inside. The town was a riot of decaying three-decker houses that sheltered screaming mothers, drunk and disorderly dads, and kids who were raised as junkyard dogs. Or at least that's what we believed about Somerville. We thought of ourselves as tough kids, but few of us would have cruised over the Somerville line on a Saturday night and stepped out of the car.

We watched the films of Somerville's first two games in our clubhouse and this time Kelly wasn't inclined to derision. "Holy shit," I believe I heard him say. "Holy shit."

He was probably talking about the tackles. Nearly everyone who talked about Somerville football that year talked about the tackles. There were two of them: hulking strong kids who played both ways. The Somerville coach was never tired of praising them. He said they were on a par with college players and maybe it wasn't fair to line them up against high school kids. He indicated that at least one of them was going to the pros. He said he'd never coached better players, or tougher ones.

Sitting on punitively hard benches in our shabby meeting room somewhere deep in the belly of Hormel Stadium, we saw the Somerville squad on film. The tackles weren't quick or all that nimble, and their approach to the game wasn't subtle. They blew you down. They especially excelled at running over the blocker on a passing play. When they were double-teamed, they ran both players over. There were plays on which four guys couldn't contain the Somerville tackles. "Holy shit." That was about right. "Holy shit."

Somerville was always tough to play. They fought you like dump rats: They scrapped and clawed and if one of their helmets came free they'd be happy to bite. The seniors finally let us know that much. Even when they had no talent, Somerville was a handful. But this year they did. They had the tackles, they had a solid quarterback, and they had strong running backs. As the head coach told us in his dry, dry way, "Somerville always has strong backs. So don't be surprised." They were stumpy fire-plugs, and in the films, we saw that they didn't dodge tacklers or take an angle away from them—they seemed to seek out op-position players so they could lower their helmets and apply the battering ram.

Malden, our Thanksgiving rival, was a city like Medford—poking its way toward middle-class respectability, or trying. Somerville was the basic mid-century urban American mess. Beating Malden was a test of skill and discipline. Beating Somerville tested guts. But we Mustangs were winners. We had an undefeated season going. Nine and 0, baby; nine and 0! Eleven and 0! Here we come.

At the center of the game of football is a religion of winning. You've got to beat the other team, knock them down, drive them off, impose your will on them. One way or another you *must* find a way to get more points than your opponent.

Is the hunger for victory stronger in football than it is in most other games? Possibly it is. A football game takes a tremendous amount of energy out of you. After a contest your body is aching in a half-dozen places and you feel you might not quite have the strength required to walk across the field and back into the club-house. Your mind is tired too: To play well, especially on offense, you have to think quickly and to good effect. And your spirit is nearly done in; you've constantly had to employ it to spark you to more and more and more effort. After a football game you're exhausted—you're exhausted even when you win. When you add losing to the equation, then all the pain is multiplied by two or three. When you think about what it feels like to lose a football game, Lombardi's famous line doesn't sound so over the top anymore: Winning isn't everything; it's the only thing.

Members of pro football teams commonly consider themselves failures if they don't make it to the Super Bowl. College squads above a certain level can feel crushed if they don't get to the national championship. It's not enough in football to have a winning season or to take your division: You're supposed to win it all. And given how much losing can hurt, it's hard not to understand why people believe all this and commit themselves to football's religion of victory.

Our assistant coaches surely did. Before the Somerville game they barked away almost as much as we did about our previous unbeaten season and the one to come. When we pounded our pads and hollered our slogans, they clapped their hands in time and hollered with us. They wanted to be part of an unbeatable football powerhouse too. Even Kelly, who had a dram of skepticism in him and had seen what he'd seen when we watched the Somerville tackles and backs in action, joined in the movement. Nine and 0! Nine and nothing! Everybody was onboard the train chugging fast to Dilboy Stadium, in Somerville.

Everybody, it seemed, but the head coach. Coach Wilson was a tall, pale, reserved man, rigid and erect as a high-church bishop. He spoke no word that he did not have to speak. It was as though every phrase was gold coin and he was hoarding for a bad day. He spoke to us mostly through the assistant coaches, who were clearly in awe of him, and through the quarterback, who was his particular charge. He could go through an entire practice standing with his clipboard in his large white hands and his whistle (which he almost never blew—whistle-blowing was for assistant coaches) around his neck and not say a single word that was aimed at the entire team. But when he did talk everyone froze; everyone listened up.

Coach Wilson clearly wasn't part of the Nine and 0 movement. When we began chanting in full-throated blasts he would walk away to the sidelines and study the holy clipboard. I believe I saw him shake his head knowingly when the assistant coaches stoked us up, like attendant priests at a rite. We players saw it and wrote it off to indifference: Coach Wilson was getting old; he'd been coaching at Medford High at least a decade and was ready to retire; he didn't really care.

If you'd looked—really looked—at the game films the Somerville coaches had sent over to us and then had a glance at our team out on the practice field, you could have stayed home and spared yourself the Medford-Somerville contest, fall 1968. What was predictable is what happened. The stronger, faster, more brutal, angrier team won. All the crap about Nine and 0 lasted through about the first quarter, and then we went into a collective crouch and took our beating. The game itself wasn't hard to anticipate; it's what happened afterward that was.

Those two big tackles had what must have been the best day of their lives. I expect that they still think back to the Medford game, smile, lift high their libation of choice, and drink it down. We simply couldn't block them. Guestie, the yes-sir and no-sir guy, our best offensive lineman, couldn't come close to handling his man. Tommy Lyons, the Brain, was a tight end on offense; there was no time to get him the ball. When our quarterback fell back to pass, it was as though someone had tossed a chunk of meat behind a flimsy fence designed to keep the wolves out. The fence broke into kindling on almost every play.

Somerville didn't simply beat us; they beat us up. One guy after another came off the field rounded down over himself, clutching an arm or a shoulder. A few limped off and stayed off, because they either couldn't move well enough to play or simply didn't want to. One or two guys got skimmed flat and into that deathlike sprawl that boxers fall into when they've been knocked onto the canvas. They got up eventually, but it took time. As for me, I didn't play at all and I didn't want to. I was safely wrapped in the cocoon of my rain cape on the sidelines, a larva with no wish to hatch and enter the dangerous world.

I saw players I held in awe fall apart. Jimmy Graham, a defensive back who looked like Little Richard and hit so hard in practice that it sounded like someone had thwacked an empty panel truck with a baseball bat, stood on the sidelines cradling his left forearm in his right and trembling. The first string quarterback sat alone looking at his hands when our defense was on the field, which was most of the time. When the call came for him to go back in, he looked up at the coach like a shell-shocked soldier ordered back to the front.

I'm not sure when the tears began. The game was certainly still going on. I saw our cocaptain Jack O'Brien, the guy who had given me those pleasurable shivers when he said Nine and 0 as I passed him in the corridor, standing alone on the sidelines. (There was a lot of standing alone on the sidelines in illustrative poses that day.) He had his helmet tipped up off his head, there was blood running lightly from his nose, and tears were sliding down his cheeks like warm rain.

This shook me. Jack was a paragon of effort and desire and toughness and all the rest, and now here he was, crying. The game meant that much to him! He cared for the game of football, he cared for Mustang football, he cared for his fellow players, and now he was showing it with tears, bitter tears. Soon almost everyone on the sidelines was crying. Soon I (who had not stepped into the game) was crying.

Anyone who only heard the soundtrack of our bus ride back to Medford would have been sure that we were returning from a funeral. There was crying and snuffling and hollers of anguish. There was some cursing, but not much. Mostly there was the sound that comes from hope being dashed, the sound that losers make: the sound of bitter, irreversible loss.

It's surprising how little good writing there is on loss and losing. Loss is such a common experience in life that you'd think it would fascinate philosophers, psychologists, and aspiring deep thinkers of all sorts. There are the poets, of course. There are brilliant poems in English about the loss not only of loved ones but of hopes, dreams, and ideals. Shelley wrote a great poem about the death of Keats, "Adonais." But he also wrote elegies for failed love affairs and his failed hopes for humanity: His last major poem, "The Triumph of Life," is a brutal record of his loss of hope for the world. But poets dramatize loss; they don't analyze its dynamics. They don't generalize about it, and neither do very many distinguished thinkers.

Part of the daring of Freud's 1917 essay "Mourning and Melancholia" is that he declines to make hard and fast distinctions between kinds of loss. He'd understand perfectly well why Shelley would write poems mourning the death of another poet and the death of his hopes for love or for salutary change in the world. Freud thought that loss is a common and nearly constant condition—maybe it's the central condition of life. We're almost always in the state of having lost something or someone that matters to us. We mourn the loss of those we love, yes—but we can also mourn our own youth and health and happiness when they are past or passing. We can also mourn when we lose in an endeavor that matters to us. We can mourn the failure of a business, the closing of a school, the failure of a political run. We can even mourn the loss of a football game.

Freud has many strong observations to make about loss and how we react to it, but there is one insight about loss and losing that's particularly rich. People react to loss in two ways, the essay says. Some people mourn, and some people lose themselves in what Freud calls "melancholia." Mourning is a process: slow, deliberate and dignified. It's a piece of demanding work. (Freud uses a German compound to describe it: *Trauerarbeit*, the work of mourning.) In mourning, each of the memories and hopes that attach us to what we've lost arises in the psyche. We remember the best times we had with the woman we loved. We recall her smile, the way the sun played off her hair, something beautifully memorable that she said. We recall these instances with a furious intensity, with a mix of pain and strange exhilaration—and then they pass away from our hearts. The process is demanding and drains the individual of a quotient of his energies. But over time, the work of mourning grows lighter, the memories become less cuttingly intense, and finally the work comes to something like an end. When it does, says Freud, "the ego becomes free and uninhibited again." That is, the individual is ready to love someone or something new.

But not everyone mourns. Some people, faced with loss, slip into melancholia. They become mad with grief. They weep and cry out against fate not only in the days that follow the loss but also in the weeks and months and sometimes even years. They will not be consoled. They will not take up the work of mourning. They simply won't let go.

If Freud had read Wordsworth, he would have seen a perfect embodiment of melancholia in a woman named Margaret, whose husband is lost to her. Margaret will not stop hoping that Robert will return—she wanders the fields and cries and sits disconsolate by her dwindling fire. She cannot care for her children.

One of them, her infant, dies because of her neglect; the other, her older boy, is taken from her to become a ward of the church parish. At one point she cries out to her friend, the elderly wise wanderer Armytage, lines that Freud would have taken in with interest. "I have slept weeping," Margaret says, "and weeping I have waked. My tears / Have flowed as if my body were not such / As others are, and I could never die."

There it is: "My tears have flowed as if my body were not such as others are." Margaret doesn't believe that she's like other people; she thinks she's special. She feels that her loss is unlike any loss that anyone has ever sustained. How could this happen to me? How could this ever happen to *me*?

Freud is a harsh moralist and he draws hard lines. There are, he says, mourners and there are melancholiacs. There are people who are sane enough to take loss and work with it, and there are those who simply can't do it. But I'm not so sure. I think that many of us can go either way when we're faced with loss. We can respond to the loss by loving and respecting what's gone and holding ourselves to the work of mourning. Or we can fall over the side the way Margaret does and give in to the mad grief (and secret narcissistic pleasures) of melancholia.

If Freud had been rattling along with us in the worn bus that took us back from Somerville's stadium to Medford, listening to the cries and snuffles, the snuffles and cries, there's not much doubt what his diagnosis would have been: melancholia, minor league. We were reacting to the loss of a game, of course—small stakes, small potatoes. But we were still showing something about ourselves. People say sports don't so much build character as reveal it. Not quite, I think. Sports reveal character so that you can (possibly) build it up. The character we revealed after the game and on the bus wasn't exactly stellar.

We were the mighty Mustangs. We were the champions. Nine and 0! Nine and 0! How, oh how could this have happened to us? How could it be? We were not such as others were. How could this have happened to *us*?

Usually on Mondays after a game, the coaches brought us together in the clubhouse room and showed us the films. We sat on our benches and Coach Wilson ran the video back and forth, using his pointer to demonstrate where matters had gone well and where we'd screwed up. The emphasis was on the screwing up. He was deliberate, patient, and abstract.

But the Monday after the Somerville game there was no film study, or "movie time," as we called it. Instead we went directly out to the practice field and were instructed to get to work. Work? At the beginning we couldn't do it. We could barely get through our calisthenics. The Medford Mustangs had passed from weeping grief to a state of collective shock. We walked around like a zombie crew, in slow motion, with no bounce or bite. We were feeling terribly, terribly sorry. We were feeling paralyzingly sorry for ourselves.

I can almost guarantee that Coach Wilson had read no philosophic reflections on mourning and loss. But he looked out at his afflicted team, made a diagnosis that the old psychoanalyst would no doubt have approved, and went to work.

The offensive line, the group of five who had burst like a dam on almost every pass play and couldn't spring a runner for most of the day, was lined up and ready to execute plays. The backs were behind them, the rest of the team clustered around, like a crowd milling outside a funeral home. Coach Wilson stepped up to the left tackle, Victor Guest (if memory serves), who had been shredded all that Saturday, and looked up into his cage. He tapped Guestie on his helmet with the flat of his palm, not hard, but enough to bring Victor into focus. Then he said something like this: "You made your man look like a hero out there Saturday. He beat you every way but sidewise." The coach paused; he stared down at the ground and let Guestie take it in. Then he peered up and into Guestie's face mask again. "You need to develop your technique—we'll be working with you on that this week. You need to work on getting lower on the pass rush. On running plays you'll need to fire off the line faster." Then another tap on the helmet. "But you're a good football player, Victor. There's no reason for you to hang your head."

Down the line Coach Wilson went, tapping each lineman on the helmet and addressing him so he could hear it clearly and so everyone else could too. He gave each guy a clear readout on his performance. He told him where he'd fallen down and where he needed to improve. He described in detail the ways each guy needed to develop. He set out plans. Then he expressed his sense, stringent as it always was, of the guy's value to the team.

Coach commended work. Don't sit hangdog; don't let yourself fall apart. Stop walking around doing the half-dead, half-living shuffle. Go to work. And take this moment as something like an opportunity. When you lose, you get a chance to learn something about your weaknesses that winners never get to learn. When you lose, you get to see something about yourself, if you can stand the view. Coach was offering the view and the guys standing shoulder-to-shoulder on the line were taking it in.

We had never heard Coach Wilson talk so much, and we'd always written his silence off to disdain or indifference. Not so, maybe. Coach waited until he had something to say, and then when he said it—no surprise—his audience was poised to hear. The assistant coaches were word factories, and after a while we only half-listened to most of them. (Kelly was the exception; he often had something memorably salty to say.) But Coach Wilson was playing the role of the wise teacher, the wise therapist of a certain sort, who bides his time and intervenes only when he's sure it will matter.

When Coach was done, the team kicked into gear and went to work—no more rah-rah; no more chanting about victories past and to come; but sober, steady work. If the coach or someone else hadn't managed to flip that switch, we might have gone on to lose our next six games running.

The coach flipped us another silver dollar's worth of advice before practice ended. "Stick together this week," he said. "When our team wins games everybody in town goes around talking about how 'We won!' When our team loses, you hear something a little different. People say, 'You lost!' It's 'We won' and it's 'You lost.' So be ready for that. Stick together and don't listen too hard to what people say." He was right about that too.

How do you get from grief to some kind of gain? You get there by tough self-assessment and then by going to work. You're going to feel terrible when you lose a football game, the way we lost to Somerville. But there is a remedy. Work lets you mourn the loss and put it behind you. Work keeps you from slipping into a permanent funk about what's happened.

Games matter in part because they don't really matter. A football game can feel like it means everything, even though on some deeper level, the level of love and loss in the actual world, it means almost nothing at all. But a football game (any game) can be a ground where we encounter life in displaced form. A good game is a *simulation* of life. There we get a chance to learn, to prepare ourselves and to grow, so when the real losses come, as they will, we may be half-ready for them. A game is a symbolic action that can get you ready for actions that are quite real.

At the time, there was plenty of real loss in my life. It had been a year or so since my sister's death and everyone in the family was taking it differently. My brother, Phil, was no doubt handling it best. When we'd arrived in Medford three years before, he'd gone out and made friends and become an outstanding student, one of those rare brainy kids other kids actually like. Phil kept on being himself, kept on thriving, though clearly he wasn't unaffected by what had happened.

My father was having his difficulties: coming home drunk more often, staying out late and playing cards, getting into the hole, borrowing, then taking call after call from collection agencies who wanted their dough *now*. I don't think he borrowed money off the street, though there was a thriving loan shark business in Medford. Those phone calls, which I often overheard, clearly made my father nervous, though I never felt he was frightened.

My father had a red-rubber-ball resilience to him. He had been used to adversity since he was young. His mother died when he was about three years old. (He told me he could remember her face, barely.) His father had remarried a woman who did not care much for my father and eventually persuaded my grandfather to send him off to live with my father's brother, George, ten years older than my father. After my father left, my grandfather and his wife had a son, to whom they gave the name Wright Aukenhead Edmundson. This was my grandfather's name, but more to the point, it was my father's name, letter for letter.

So my father bounced around from his brother's house to one of his sisters' and back again. How he managed to finish high school and learn to play the flute (which he put aside after I was born) and find a job and stay mostly solvent is not easy to say. But he did it. When my sister died, my father drank more, gambled more, caroused more, but he never quite jumped the tracks and ended up in jail or punched out in an alley.

My mother took Barbara Ann's death the hardest. Often when we were watching TV at night, she would stand up and go to the bedroom, close the door, and push her head into her pillow and cry. When I went to her, she would look up, try to clear her tears, and say, simply, "I'm sad about the baby. There's nothing you can do."

My mother was a child of the Depression. The salient memory of her childhood was of the day her father, whom she adored, lost his job driving a truck. She walked in from school to see him sitting on the couch in the living room with his head in his hands, weeping. My grandfather was a stoic Yankee and she had never seen him cry. The next years of my mother's life were spent in poverty or near-poverty. When her father went off with his fishing rod in the morning, he was fishing for their dinner. If he didn't catch anything, they ate oatmeal, or whatever cereal they'd had for breakfast. My mother grew up amid sorrow (though she dearly loved and was loved by her sister and her mother), and now with my sister's death sorrow was back with redoubled force.

There was a photograph of my sister in the living room— Barbara Ann with her luminous blue eyes, fair skin, and an expression that seemed more frightened and confused the more you looked at it. Though she was a beautiful child in her way, her beauty was deceiving: Her mind wasn't right; she couldn't speak; she walked dragging her leg. On the wall was a reproduction of Renoir's *A Girl with a Watering Can*. My mother had chosen it from a catalog, redeeming books and books of S&H Green Stamps for it not long after Barbara Ann got sick. The picture shows a tender young girl in her garden—healthy, sweet, and perfectly happy.

There was a crucifix in my parents' bedroom, a heavy mahogany cross with a gold image of Jesus affixed. It must have weighed three or four pounds. When my mother passed it, she often looked up and murmured a few words. I listened and listened to find out what they were. One day I heard her: "Lord give me strength. Dear Lord Jesus, give me strength."

She meant strength to keep going, I'm sure. She needed all she could muster to keep cooking our meals and cleaning our clothes and pulling the house together. She needed strength to deal with my father when he came home drunk, or to deal with her own anger and fear when he didn't come home at all. Was he hurt? Had he been in an accident? (My father would drive his car when he could only half-walk.) She would call his job to try to find out where he was. And yes—he was there at his desk, had been since six that morning, working away.

Lord Jesus, give me strength. As Catholics, we believed that Jesus had chosen his suffering and death voluntarily to redeem our sins and the sin of Adam. He did not have to accept the cross. "Jesus was God, children," a nun at Sacred Heart Church told us. "Jesus was *God*! At any time he wanted to during his crucifixion he could have blinked an eye and sent those Roman soldiers tumbling down the hill like toys. He could have stepped off the cross and walked away anytime he liked." But Jesus did not, and he didn't because he chose not to. He chose to stay on the cross and suffer for you and you and you and me.

There was a way out of my mother's predicament, no doubt about it. She could have come off the cross. She could have done it by letting go and breaking down. She could have started crying one night after dinner and not stopped. "I have slept weeping," Wordsworth's Margaret says, "and weeping I have waked." My mother could have done exactly what Margaret did and let everything go, quit the work of mourning, and embraced raging grief. There were times when I'm sure that she was close. Soon she would have been in a hospital and what would have happened to the three of us when she went is anyone's guess. But my mother didn't break down and let it all drop, though she must have been sorely tempted by the prospect. She took care of her kids and she took care of her wayward husband, or tried. She did the work of mourning and the work of keeping us together.

I at least half-understood what Coach Wilson was doing when he went down the line tapping helmets and talking about work and trying to bring us Mustangs back to the tasks before us. We'd lost and that was too bad. But no one was going to get to wallow in it. No one was going to be defined by one meager effort in a big game. The coach worked his quotidian magic, pushing us all out of our gotten-up adolescent melancholia and back into the world of football, where we could shed our sorrow through work. Good for him. Good for him. He showed us that a football education can help you begin to learn a lesson that's as valuable as most any: how to lose.

The poet Elizabeth Bishop begins a wonderful villanelle on loss with the simple phrase "The art of losing isn't hard to master." But Bishop is mocking herself, and mocking all others who think they know everything there is to know about loss. It's an impossible art to master, losing, but a game like football can begin to teach you something about how to lose. You lose a football game in a safe, defined environment, where the game means everything but also nothing. You feel the loss—it's bitter as iron in your mouth. But what they say on the playground is true: It's only a game. In football you get to rehearse life before you play it out for mortal stakes, which is part of what makes the game as valuable as it is.

Guys who've played football can become victory junkies. After they play football, everything is about wins and losses. In whatever they do—get married, start a business, raise kids—they have to figure out a way to compete and to win. And that means, naturally, that someone else has to lose. They spend their lives thinking of themselves and, maybe worse, thinking of others as winners or as losers. They're constantly immersed in a war of each against all. Football hasn't been an elixir to them but a species of poison.

But other guys get their first experience of losing on a football field, and if they have a coach as shrewd as mine was, they get to figure out a lot about themselves and about the world. They get to learn something about how to lose. They figure out how to assess the situation, take stock of their weaknesses, look ahead, and go to work. They learn something about how to mourn.

A genuinely profound lesson about loss and mourning was there in front of my eyes every day, of course, brought to me by my mother. Her courage was displayed not in a game—in a world of symbolic action—but in the harsh actual world, for which even the most serious schooling can only partially prepare us. I was young and self-absorbed—I couldn't take in the lesson as it unfolded day by day, meal by meal, laundry load by load in front of my eyes. Maybe it was because as a guy—a guy born in the fifties, no less—I could only learn from other men and was dully immune to the wisdom women embodied and dispensed. Maybe wisdom conveyed through a game is more accessible because of the way a game shrinks and intensifies the world—somewhat the way a book or a work of art can do.

It took me years to see what my mother had accomplished and to express the appropriate gratitude. For there it was: fortitude, determination, deep mourning that never tipped over into ruining melancholia, and the fulfillment of the Christian ideal, the emulation of the compassionate and suffering Teacher.

4

THE BLIND-BACKER:
CHARACTER TIMES TWO

During the summer between my junior and senior years, I went on a self-improvement kick. I did all I could to get myself in shape for football. That spring a sample edition of a magazine had arrived at my house. It was called *The Well-Conditioned Athlete*, or something like that. I'd never seen a fitness magazine before and did not know they existed. I was enthralled. *The Well-Conditioned Athlete* laid out a half-dozen or so plans for getting into better shape. Naturally, I took the most strenuous and found myself running through my neighborhood at all hours and training with the milers on the track team from time to time. I lifted weights too. I'd gotten my parents to buy me 150 pounds of plates and a bar, and often when the apartment was empty, I stripped down to my shorts and spent an hour or so doing every exercise *The Well-Conditioned Athlete* recommended.

The Athlete was strong on diet too. I had never considered the possibility that what I ate might have a bearing on my strength and endurance. I ate what was around. I ate what my mother served: meat and potatoes and vegetables. But I also ate what was in stock at the local variety store, the Spa. I was happy to throw down Ring Dings and Twinkies and apple pies that contained more white sugar than apples. I liked candy bars too and was often disposed to pick up two or three and dispatch them in close sequence. My favorite after-school snack was two jelly dough-nuts and a Coke. You could buy that treat at the time for some-where around thirty-five cents.

After I read my one issue of *The Athlete* this changed. I read only the one issue because the thought of actually subscribing to a magazine was beyond me—that was something grown-ups did. Also, magazine subscription was a fraught subject in my house. When I was five or six, my parents paid for a year's sub-scription to *Life* magazine—but only for a year's. After the first fifty-two or so issues, *Life* kept coming (as it will), even follow-ing us from Malden to Medford. But no bills arrived. Sometimes we reveled in what appeared to be our great good fortune. Other times, my mother fretted aloud that *Life* might send a represen-tative to the door to demand back payment. My father? He merely expressed the wish that he be around when the collector from *Life* rang the buzzer: My father had much to impart about the magazine and about its subject, too. So I did not subscribe to *The Well-Conditioned Athlete*, but read and reread my one copy until it began turning to pulp.

I stopped eating my doughnuts and drinking my Coke—or at least I did less of that. I also got fixated on the idea of supplements. I pored over the pages advertising complex muscle-building, endurance-enhancing pills. I took an interest in seaweed capsules and vitamins with extra iron. But what I finally battened on to was wheat germ. I decided that consuming wheat germ would make me faster and stronger, and all the rest. Also, wheat germ was cheap. I came home from the nearest health food store, which I had to go three towns over to find, with a plastic tub full of it.

I put it on everything. I put wheat germ on my cereal, wheat germ on my ice cream, wheat germ on my potatoes. If my mother had not stopped me, I would have buried my meat and vegetables in wheat germ. I made concoctions out of wheat germ and yogurt and milk and I chugged them down. Wheat germ tastes like sawdust. But I was persuaded that the worse my supplement tasted, the more it would do for me. So lay on the wheat germ!

When summer came and school ended I tried to get my conditioning life going full throttle. But there was a problem: I had a job—or, rather, I had a job that was not a job. Every morning I piled half-asleep into my father's rusted-out Cadillac and headed off with him to the factory where he worked. I had a summer job at Raytheon in Bedford, up Route 128. It was a summer job that all my friends envied: it was a well-paying (way above minimum wage), clean (I worked in an office), steady job at which I did nothing at all.

My father had managed to get me hired but there was no work for me to do. Day after day, I sat eight hours straight in a downstairs office at Raytheon alongside a wooden table in the company of two other guys about my age. Their dads were big-wigs in the company; they had their offices on the top floor. How my father scored me a piece of patronage on this level, I couldn't say. He was known as an all-around good guy at the plant, although, as a few of his coworkers told me, he thought he was smarter than everyone else.

My two young colleagues and I had nothing to do. Our so-called supervisor could not come up with any tasks for us other than filling out our weekly hour and pay report, which we did in the most excruciating details. We had nothing to do, but we could not do nothing. We had to look busy. We could not read books, we could not talk in anything but a whisper, we could not use the phone, and we could not look at a newspaper. We brought in papers from home and pretended to consult them; we played games of tic-tac-toe and hangman, clandestinely sliding the paper back and forth, then regarding it as though it were a significant legal document. We went off on what we called safaris—protracted walks around the plant, which could go on for an hour or more. It was understood that two of us had to stay at the desk to hold down the fort that was not really a fort. Safaris were much desired and we kept mental lists not only of who had walked the last one and the one before, but how long the explorer had been gone.

Melville's Bartleby, the most famous disaffected office worker in literature, does no work because he "would prefer not to." We would have much preferred having something to do, but Raytheon did not provide it, so mostly we sat silently and thought our thoughts.

My thoughts were almost all focused on the gym. After work I would find a way to get to Malden, the city I'd been born in, where there was a YMCA. Sometimes my father drove me—but frequently he had activities to attend to after work. Often I got a ride with my dad's friend George, who lived in the other direction from us but loved driving around and would do anything for a buddy. His car was in even worse shape than my father's: Its floor was littered with cigarette butts and beer cans. As soon as we got into the vehicle in the Raytheon parking lot, George lit a cig and popped a Bud Tall Boy. He was good-natured and kind and, like my father, a gambler. George won, though. When he opened his wallet I saw an inch-thick roll of twenties and tens. My father told me that George made so much money gambling that he often forgot to cash his Raytheon checks. When we rolled out of the parking lot, George raised his Tall Boy out the window and offered a toast to the guy in the security booth.

George drove slowly, puffing his smokes and savoring his beer. Sometimes he managed to kill a pair of Tall Boys by the time we got to Malden and the YMCA. Occasionally his daughter accompanied us—she was about twenty years old and had blond hair and wore frighteningly red lipstick. She adored George, encouraging him when he told stories and when he decided to drive the car exclusively with his knees so he could better attend to the butt and the beer.

The car cruised to the curb outside the Y and George often asked me to hop out while it was still slightly rolling, since doing so would improve my agility. In a few minutes I was inside the Y, changed into my gym clothes, and headed for the weight room, to get myself ready for senior year football. I was determined to grow strong.

I loved that weight room. It was everything a 1969 weight room at a YMCA in a working-class city would predictably be. It was subbasement, dank, small, mildly foul smelling, and low ceilinged; the lights were fluorescent, the floor concrete and scuffed. But there was a terrific collection of free weights, hundreds and hundreds of pounds with multiple bars (in a few different designs), racks upon racks of dumbbells, a frame and brace for doing squats, and of course the most important implement of all, the bench. There were two benches, actually, the little and the big. And naturally, there was a hierarchy.

The big bench was the property of the bruisers, guys in their twenties and early thirties who showed up daily at the Y, usually after work, as I did. There they met their partners, who spotted them on the bench, and they went to work. Rotation order was scrupulously observed and enforced. When you finished your set, you hopped off double-quick and gave the spot to the next guy up.

I was, from day one, big-bench material, but only barely. I could work with two hundred pounds and that's what it took to qualify. No big-bencher would ever lift on the little bench, and woe betide a little-bencher who tried to go beyond his rank and station. To accommodate the little-bencher, you had to slide off too many plates, which slowed everything down. And of course the little-benchers were, well . . . they were little. Two hundred was the starting point—guys loaded it up way beyond. But if you couldn't handle the two, you had to go little bench.

A harsh atmosphere, toxic with manly competitiveness? Hardly. When you were on the bench you had the attention of most of the other lifters, and when you got to your repetition limit, which everyone gleaned within a week of your arrival, the room would be rooting for you to surpass it. "One more, c'mon. C'mon, one more." Your partner would put a light hand under the bar as you sweated and strained and often screamed in an agony of pain and pleasure. "You can do it! You can do it!" If someone surpassed his usual number of reps or shot a vast weight up once off his chest, the smelly cellar resounded with clapping and hoots.

I became a student of weight training, passing beyond my one flayed issue of *The Athlete*, which had only an article or two on the subject, and heading off to the library (a site little-known to me previously) to cop books on the art of building strength with weights. There was a right way and a wrong way, it turned out. Muscles grew by being put under intense pressure, so much pressure that you broke them down; then you had to rest to let them reconstitute themselves. In doing so, they'd become larger and more potent than they were before. Rest was as important as activity, it turned out. And you had to know what kind of strength you were building. If I had been preparing for the shot put, I would have wanted to do one or two reps with the heaviest weight I could handle. If I wanted to be a distance swimmer, it would be lots of reps with lighter weights. (I didn't want to be a swimmer, not at all. My first experience in the water had been at the age of six, when I'd been tossed naked into a pool with a hundred other naked thrashing six-year-olds. The pool had been the one here at the Y. It was across the hall from the weight room, and when I went downstairs and smelled the chlorine and the funk, I flashed back to the swimming lesson, which had become my image of what it would be like on the first day of hell: naked screaming people, shoving and crying, though maybe the authorities would substitute fire for water.) My weight program was something between the swimmer's and the shot-putter's, though closer to the shot-putters, naturally. I aimed for six or eight reps and as many sets as I could sustain. On Monday, Wednesday, and Friday I worked upper body; Tuesday and Thursday were all about legs. Then I locked myself into the squat machine and ducked up and down with three hundred pounds and more secured on my back. Then upstairs for running—a few miles around the track and sprints up and down the basketball court, which no one seemed to use for basketball.

When I got home—sometimes my father got me; sometimes George swung by, six beers in but seemingly none the worse— I was deliciously tired. I collapsed on my bed and turned on WMEX (pop rock) and stared in blissful emptiness at the ceiling. I had transported myself to lotus land.

If there is any feeling better than having worked your body

hard with a strong goal in mind, I'm not sure what it is. When I finished a workout at the Y, I felt like I'd erased the blackboard. I'd washed it down. All the layers of thought and feeling, the nibblings of conscience (or the outright devouring bites—the agenbite of inwit, as James Joyce calls it) disappear. The worries and the hopes and even the affections and dislikes are all gone, and you simply are. It's as close as you can come to an everyday, nothing-special rebirth, and I treasured it. I'm not alone, of course—people run and swim and when they get old they walk for all they're worth, so as to arrive at this well-earned lotus bath of contentment. It feels good when you do it at the behest of a coach and in the company of a team. But somehow it feels better when you do it by yourself and because you want to. You can quit anytime you like, when the bar gets too heavy, or the last phase of the suicide drill makes you feel you are going to collapse—but instead of quitting you push on. And then you're done—done when you say you're done, because you've achieved all you had in mind for the day. Feels good.

And when you've found that zone of honest, devoted exhaustion and learned its pleasures, then you have a resource that will be with you for the rest of your life. It's hard; it hurts—but you'll always know how to throw yourself in, erase the board teeming with squiggles and swirls and way too many exclamation points to be comfortable, and start again. Football gave me that process indirectly. A self-imposed workout is Western meditation at its finest—not tranquil Zen breaths, but all-American panting and puffing, followed by a peace that may be as fine in its way as anything the monks can produce with two hours of concentrated oms amid the tinkling of bells.

After football, exercise—often exercise that brought me to blissful exhaustion—became a constant part of my life. Almost every day I looked for, and still look for, a way to get out and go. Football got me into exercise before there was a movement. When, in the summer after I graduated from college, I lived for a while on the Upper East Side of New York (rent-free), I ran daily around the reservoir in Central Park—two, three, four times. This was 1974. I was never quite alone during my runs: There were dog walkers and strollers and now and then a fellow runner. But there were not many. (Now it can look like the subway has emptied out and a crowd is bustling home double-quick.) I was having a rough time, just out of college, low on cash, low on prospects. The running helped keep me whole, until some cash and some prospects turned up (in their own sweet time). I'm not sure I knew it then, but the salutary running was part of my football legacy, a gift from the Mustang coaches, the gang at the Y, and the editors of *The Well-Conditioned Athlete*, arriving just in time to help me out.

My high school workout regimen had another dimension too. The regimen and the Y were making me a student, though not a student of history or philosophy, or physics. I was becoming a student of my own body. I was using knowledge and observation to figure out how to develop. I was athlete (kind of) and trainer at the same time. I was sculptor (kind of) and knotholed, splintery block of wood. I had to draw up plans for getting stronger and faster; I had to put them in action, evaluate my progress, then revise and revise. I was compelled to do this by myself, with no one much to talk with about it. My father thought I was nuts spending time in a smelly gym when there was beer to drink, cigarettes to smoke, TV to watch, and cards to play. Though he was terribly kind in getting me to the Y and back. Still, he was never quite ready for a discussion on whether I should up my reps or my poundage, or whether wheat germ was really all it was cracked up to be. I never wrote term papers; I never did the lab experiments in science; I never drew and then redrew a picture. My football workout program was my first foray into setting up a routine and working on it and revising the work, and *finally* getting somewhere with it. By the end of the summer I was way stronger and even a little faster than I had been.

And of course my exercise program became a template for every other endeavor of the same sort in future life. Each time I've had the wherewithal to plan ahead and set myself to work on a project that required more than a two-step, I had the example of my YMCA workouts and my football prep to look back to. When I applied to college and applied to grad school and worked on essays and, in time, on that frustrating dissertation, I had a pattern for how it was to be done. I taught myself that almost nothing good happens fast, except maybe for winning the lottery—though we're told that, in the long run, lottery winning makes more people miserable than not. (Try me, I say.) Bad things happen fast: The brakes give out; the stroller goes bouncing down the steps; the lump of gristle sticks in your throat (and sticks). Good things are all about progress: effort, expectation, and desire, and something evermore about to be, as the poet says.

When I earned my uniform and became at home in it, I began to develop character. True enough. But when I was able to throw myself into that Y program, I did more than begin. On the field, I had the coaches driving me on; at the Y, I had my bench-press buddies, but most of the work was up to me. I became my own coach. I was a demanding coach who didn't take many excuses and who asked a lot from the player, who was also himself, and by the end of the summer player and coach showed that they could collaborate to create something that mattered: a me that was more than me. I went at it hard. I spent myself strongly that summer. You might say I moved up to the second degree of character building. I spent myself full out, but as Robert Frost tells us, "strongly spent is synonymous with kept."

However.

However. One of the guys who hung out in the weight room was Coach Kelly's older brother (or maybe a cousin; I'm not sure). He was a swimmer, very fit, as good-looking as Kelly, but he seemed to take life a tad more easily. He was one of the two or three presiding and benevolent alphas there in the cave. One day, as I was rolling off the bench, he asked me about my glasses. My glasses were thick, probably yellowed at the rims, perhaps mildly cracked in one lens. Did I say thick? They were the kind of glasses you torched anthills with, if you were so inclined. They looked like you could use them to bring down fire from the sky and give the ants the Sodom and Gomorrah treatment.

"How do you play football," the Brother said, "with those glasses on?"

I told the Brother that I took them off and handed them to the team manager at the beginning of practice and games. When something required close attention, I called for my specs, much as I called for my inhaler when my lungs went tight and I began to wheeze. (Y. A. Tittle's teammates recalled that their own trainers seemed weighed down with all of Tittle's wheeze-prevention paraphernalia.) If the coach diagrammed a play: Glasses! Otherwise it was me squinting and groping to try to figure out who was who and what was what. I was pretty good at this, but at least once I mixed matters up and KO'd a guy on my own squad. And I mean KO'd—I ran into him and knocked him cold.

"You're blind as a bat," the Brother said. I agreed that this was true.

"If you can't see, you can't really play ball," he continued. I wanted to protest, but this was Coach's brother (or cousin, or something).

"You need sports glasses," he told me. "You've got to get yourself a pair of sports glasses."

There was a kid on our team who wore sports glasses. His name was Tony Spindolini and he lived up to it. He was a puny, spindly, spiderlike guy, who hopped in at halfback all the time and could be brought down by a sudden strong breeze. He was also amiably self-aware and quite funny, but that mattered a bit less. Tony wore sports glasses, double-thick panes framed with putty-colored plastic. To accommodate the sports glasses, he had an ugly, jutting face mask. Somehow it made him look like a spaceman. Tony did not look cool, not at all. Tony looked like Atom Ant, and that's what we called him: Atom-Fucking-Ant.

I had a far better (albeit very occasionally applied) nickname: Ben, for my purported resemblance to the Oakland Raiders' fierce defensive lineman Ben Davidson. I wasn't Atom-Fucking-Ant. I was Ben-Fucking-Davidson. I did not wish to be Atom Ant's big brother. I wanted to look cool. When I went back to football I was determined to cop one of the helmets with the major cages, one like the Brain had worn.

I was gaining weight, putting on muscle, picking up speed. Day by day, I was getting more Brain-like and less Ant-ish. But Atom Ant had one advantage over me: Atom Ant could see. He could take in what was going on when he was on the field. It didn't do him much good: He got planted anyway. But he could actually see.

When the Brother brought up the sports glasses, I closed down. I didn't want to hear it. Going Atom Ant was not part of my plan. Going Atom Ant was not what sent me to the gym five and sometimes six days a week to puff and grunt and groan as though I were in labor and about to give birth—to a new self, of course. A new self!

Some of my teammates had told me the same thing Big Kelly did, albeit in a more compressed way. One of their nicknames for me was the All-Pro Blind-Backer. All the insight I needed was there, packed into that nickname. That is: You'd really be pretty good if you could see. I preferred Ben.

I thought and I planned. I read and studied. I kept a notebook with records of my progress. How much did I bench on August 3, 1969? How much did I hoist in the military press? (That was really my strongest exercise.) I knew because I put it all down. I was devoted and admirably determined. But the one piece of advice that could have given me a real chance to achieve what I wanted to and become a topflight ballplayer was completely lost on me. I shrugged off what Big Kelly said and that was that. I didn't hear it, or couldn't hear it, or didn't want to. I was a little like the guy in the joke who prays and prays to the Lord on high that he'll let him win the lottery. He fasts and he prays; he prays and he fasts. And he's constantly upbraiding the Lord for never coming through for him. Says the Lord one day, sick of all the malarkey: "Buddy, why don't you try buying a ticket?" My prayers came in the form of sweat and effort and strain, and as a sort of reward for my devotion the gods of football visited me with some sage advice: Get some sports glasses. Buy a ticket.

Sports gods, I ignored you. Lords of the Gridiron, I am truly sorry I did not heed your injunctions—I think.

But why didn't I? It was right in front of me, really. I would have had to overcome a small dose of vanity, but what was that? (Does Freud ever talk about face mask envy?) Getting a pair of sports glasses and a spaceman helmet with a jutting shield on the front would not have taken care of all my difficulties. It wouldn't have made me any faster afoot. (Speed is hard to develop.) And sports glasses wouldn't have made my reaction time all that much quicker: In football, as in all areas of life, I usually look before I leap, and then look again and sometimes pause to compose an abbreviated essay. Nothing would have changed that. But with sharp vision I would have had a fighting chance on the football team. I might actually have been quite good.

I was willing to sweat and strain like a country mule all that summer in pursuit of a goal, but I couldn't take the one simple, sincere piece of advice that might have closed the deal for me. I could work and work, but I couldn't see the truth in front of me. I was, as it were, blind to my blindness.

I got in my own way. I tripped over my feet. I screwed myself up. Looking back, that much is clear. I blew it.

But don't we all—or don't most of us, at least some of the time? We've all got our blind spots, though usually they aren't quite as literal as mine was. We can see a splinter in our neighbor's eye and miss the log that's lodged (somehow or other) in our own. There are lots of illuminating definitions of what it is to be a human being. A human is the political animal, says Aristotle; the rational animal, says Plato (in a very upbeat mood); the language animal, suggests Noam Chomsky; the inventor of the negative, says an ingenious Kenneth Burke. I might tentatively and with due modesty add a definition to the bottom of the list: The human being is the animal that doesn't (and maybe can't) quite know itself. He's the creature with the blind spot, though it's not always myopia pure and simple.

The guy across from you at the wedding can't stand his mother, sitting to his left at the table, and he doesn't know it; your buddy who works all day, every day on his novel was not designed by God or muses to write novels, but he'd kill 'em with a nonfiction work; the moping investment banker has the heart of a schoolteacher, and the schoolteacher needs worlds to conquer far beyond the boundaries of K–12. These matters aren't terribly hard to discern. Carl Jung said once that any truly perceptive person who simply watched you walking down a crowded street could tell you secrets about yourself that it would take you years of psychoanalysis to unlock.

But if that perceptive observer told you, you wouldn't listen. Who the hell are you to tell me my business? Bug off. Bugger away. So if I imparted my perception about mom hating, or nonfiction writing, or breaking out of the K–12 gulag, my interlocutor probably wouldn't hear a word. If I persisted, I expect I might earn nothing better than a pop in the nose.

I didn't punch Big Kelly in the nose—he was Big Kelly. But I didn't hear a word, really. Didn't take it in. I pictured myself as Atom Ant Senior, disliked the picture, and let it fade to white.

Why did I do this? Why do we? Is it because we're so guilty over past offenses that we don't want to possess the best that our lives might offer us? Are we atoning for some sins past or to come by not rising high in the world, or as high as we might? Maybe we simply, and not entirely irrationally, fear success because we do not know how we will handle it and what it might do to us. Was there (maybe, maybe) something in me that knew that had I become a football hero or something like one, I would have become more aggressive, more belligerent, more cocksure, maybe smacked someone in the mouth and gotten myself in real trouble; maybe gotten myself a football player's girlfriend and gotten her pregnant?

No, no, not quite. That's all too literal. But I do think that maybe there was something in me that wanted to preserve my position as a semi-outsider. I liked being both in and out of the game. I rarely liked being in the swim, jumping full force into the salmon falls and the mackerel-crowded sea and splashing around there. (Not for nothing did I see that moment of YMCA all-in naked swim as a foretaste of hell.) I was born a bit of an old fella, a little like Falstaff, maybe, who claims to have come out of the womb with a white head and something of a round belly. My football blindness kept me on the sidelines where I maybe wanted and needed to be. Who knows? Stranger things have been true.

My grad school prof Paul de Man wrote an influential book in which he claimed that legitimate philosophical insights were often enabled by blindness. The inability to see a truth that was all too obvious allowed certain writers to see truths that were far less obvious but more consequential. Tiresias, the Greek seer, was blind. But not being mesmerized by outward appearances seems to have allowed him to see into the heart of life. The same may have been true for Homer (depicted as blind) and Oedipus (who really begins to know himself when he puts out his eyes). So then, is the human being the animal who knows (on whatever level) that knowing himself could be particularly detrimental?

For whatever it may be worth, had I gotten those sports glasses I'd probably never have written this book.

Who can say? I came to my realization about being blind to my football blindness after I had sat for fifteen minutes with a fortune-teller on something called a Psychic Sail. The voyage took place during that summer when I was living in New York and jogging without much company to speak of every day around the reservoir. A ship was loaded up with tarot readers and palmists and swamis of all stripes, and sailed around the island of Manhattan. The fortune-tellers generated insights into the guests and then, when they were through with us, went to work on each other. (There were some marvelous spats.) I covered this event (if event it was) for the *Village Voice*.

I got my fortune told a half-dozen times, and mostly it was off the wall. (I was going to go on plenty of long journeys. I asked if the Psychic Sail qualified as a long journey and received knowing smiles.) But one palmist seemed to have my number. She was one of those people Jung talks about who see you walking down the street and know you better than you know yourself, at least in part. At the end of my reading she peered up at me from under her turban and she said: "You could be a great success in life, but something in you doesn't want that to happen."

Not much later I thought of Big Kelly and the weight room and the big bench and the record keeping and the damned sports glasses. And I vowed to myself that whenever I went after anything in the future, I would listen to what people told me on the way, even if it seemed beside the point, and that I'd look out for my blind spot, the way I do when I'm changing lanes in a car. (My wife's station wagon has an amber light that goes off when something enters the blind spot. If only.) So I'm constantly on the job seeking out my blind spots. I try to listen to what I don't want to hear. I try to listen, maybe, for what I cannot hear. But has my vigilance worked? Can I do now what my seventeen-year-old self couldn't? And would it be good if I could, given what Professor de Man told me about the virtues of blindness and what I've maybe discovered myself? What's better, blindness or insight?

I'm not sure. Maybe I'd be the last one you should ask.

5

SPIRIT IN THE SKY: PATRIOTISM

One day at practice behind Hormel Stadium, something strange appeared in the sky. I can date the event with some precision. It was October 15, 1969, a Wednesday. Suddenly what was going on with us Medford Mustangs was about to intersect, if just slightly, with major events in the world. And I was about to take another step in my football education.

I was a senior now. It was my second year playing ball, and the whole experience of the game had changed for me. It wasn't that I'd become a star—nothing like that had happened or would. I was still going to do a lot more watching of the games than playing in them. After the opening kickoff, when I was usually on the field, I could be found sitting on the long splinter-filled bench, blue cape over my shoulders if it was cold, helmet tilted back on my head, legs straight out, taking in the ball game. So I was a benchwarmer, a pine rider. And mostly I disliked it. I wanted to play; I wanted to play all the time. But in another part of myself, I was pleased to be on the periphery, taking in the show and thinking a little about it from time to time. I liked being "both in and out of the game and watching and wondering at it," as the poet says.

I was enrolled in a philosophy class with a brilliant teacher, Franklin Lears, and slowly (*very* slowly) the world of thought was opening up to me. I didn't read much, not yet. But the questions that my teacher was asking were beginning to take hold. What is goodness? What is justice? Why does Plato think that it is better to receive harm than to do it? This last question was particularly tough for my football player self to handle. Was it really better to receive harm than to commit it? Better to get hit than hit? Better to be knocked on your butt than to do the knocking? But the teacher admired Plato, and without quite knowing it, the class began to admire the persistent, ironic teacher who posed these impossible questions.

Still, my main identity was as a football player. On the day the spirit in the sky appeared, I could claim to be a hard-core member of the team. I was well accepted by the other players. I had a quotient of football-based character: Over time I'd become more and more like that guy in the mirror, well padded and close to being at one with himself. I'd developed some football courage too, but the quality of my courage had changed. Sometimes I would still throw myself into a rage by flashing back on a bitter image or summoning my magic (black magic) words. But now, I often didn't have to amp myself into overdrive to throw a decent block or stick my head in on a tackle. I was used to doing those things, and they didn't hurt as much as they looked like they did. It hurt more when you didn't go at the game full tilt. Then you were a victim, not an initiator. So what had begun in something like hysteria had become closer to habit.

I hung out with the team stars (who were actually rather kindly guys) and I lorded it (gently) over the juniors and the sophomores on the squad. I was a made man, though I inhabited a modest-enough rung.

And of course I'd spent the summer before lifting those weights at the Malden YMCA. I could bench nearly 250—the gold standard at the time for a high school lineman. (Not now. Two-fifty now is close to a joke.) I didn't wake up in the night whimpering after a hard practice as I had my junior year. I didn't look down the line when we went one-on-one to make sure I'd be matched up with a guy I could handle. Why didn't I play more? I was slow; I of course was nearsighted. I was the All-Pro Blind-Backer who couldn't see his way to a pair of sports glasses. Also, I sometimes decided that the assignment for blocking or pass coverage that the coaches had drawn up didn't take all factors into account and modified it to suit myself.

We'd had a mediocre season my junior year, five wins and four defeats. After the Somerville loss, we'd pulled ourselves together, much thanks to the head coach's hard-edged therapy. Still, we hadn't managed much of a season.

On the day of the airborne event, we Mustangs were playing brilliantly. We were undefeated: 3 and 0. (Though we didn't do much chanting about it.) We'd overcome Boston Latin in a tight game, rolled over Chelsea, and then gone and actually beaten Somerville. Somerville still had a raging defense, and I'm not sure we blocked them that much better than we had the year before. But our backs pulled us through. We had a racehorse of a fullback, who was healthy only rarely, but he was in top form for Somerville. At the close of the game he leapt over one of Somerville's fierce linebackers to score a touchdown—he looked like a guy clearing a hurdle. When our back made it into the end zone, the linebacker was still standing there frozen. And our quarterback had a spectacular day, running and throwing and running again. When backs are on like that, a little blocking goes a long way.

Still, it took a wobbly, dying duck of an extra point to win it: 21 to 20. We'd come from behind. We'd taken them. After the extra point we grabbed Coach Wilson and mounted him on our shoulders and carried him, pharaoh-like, to the locker room. His facial expression as he bobbed atop his celebrating ballplayers suggested he'd downed a double shot of vinegar. When we finally put him down close by the showers, he mounted a bench and gave his postgame speech. It went something like this: "Now you see what can happen if you stick with a thing and don't give up." That was the speech from beginning to end. Coach was determined to help us take victories in stride too. I particularly like the "what can happen": Do what you like, stick in all you can—still there are no guarantees. In later life I've repeated Coach Wilson's words to myself a few times; they actually seem to work better than trumpets and drums.

On the day the spirit in the sky appeared we were getting ready for a game with North Quincy—and we were loose and happy and very sure of ourselves.

October 15 was a glorious day. The sky was clear, the color of the ocean on a soft, sunlit afternoon. For some reason we were taking it easy at practice. We weren't throwing ourselves into each other or banging the blocking sled around the edges of the field, pushing like mules, trying to plow a stony pasture that was never going to get plowed. We were running plays in slow motion. We were learning a set of offensive alignments and executions designed especially for North Quincy and we were doing it in a surprisingly mellow way.

Up in the sky over our heads there appeared an airplane and it began to eject smoke—not black, impending-disaster smoke, but white frothy stuff: lamb-gentle, cloudlike. The smoke stayed where it was. It didn't fade. It was as though the plane was a giant piece of chalk moved by an invisible hand. The plane flew slowly, slowly, taking its time. Whose hand held the chalk? Who had commissioned the plane? We'd all seen skywriting. It tended to be commercial. Sunbeam bread! Hood milk! But the scope of this effort was larger. Soon there was a half-moon curve, a white scythe shape in the sky.

Now it had our attention. It was like the bee that floats in through the crack of the open classroom window and mesmerizes the kids who are supposed to be grinding away at their geometry, contemplating the beauties of the side-angle-side theorem. But the bee is floating its heavy yet weightless float through the classroom, on a desultory tour, not looking for anything, in no hurry to leave. The teacher thwacks at it once or twice with a rolled-up paper, and each time she does, she springs back in fear that she tries to pass off as mock fear. The bee is unimpressed and floats its solitary float. The kids stare at it with half-open mouths, as though it were a hypnotist's coin spinning in front of their eyes. Before you know it, the teacher has given up pretenses and has locked on to the bee herself. Everyone in the room has evacuated responsibility and identity and slipped into a sort of time lazily outside of time. And for a while, everyone is something not unlike happy.

So on the football field we drifted lazily through our drills, but we let the flight of the airplane and the shape it was creating take us over. I was going in every third play—that's what the backups did—so I had plenty of time to watch and wonder. We entered something like a collective dream. Even the coaches, who were usually in wakeful overdrive, seemed to feel the beckoning of the white ghostly script, now forming a colossal wreath in the sky. It looked like a huge smoke ring, as though Vulcan or Zeus were puffing a fat cigar and had sent the first of what might be many weightless ovals into space.

It's a Hula Hoop! It's a necklace! It's a zero—like you! (Ha ha.) We guessed, but even the guesses came off lazily, as though we'd been transported and were playing now not on the bricklike soil of the stadium practice field, with its tiny scrubs of defiant, browned grass here and there, like pathetic oases, but as though we were in a meadow of poppies, like the one that Dorothy and her friends cross on their way to Oz, the meadow that leaves them all snoozing like cats in the sun. Now the shape was a vast empty eye in the blue and we stared into it and were made, if possible, even quieter. If the coaches had demanded one-on-ones or grass drills, we might have fallen down laughing, and rolled like puppies on the ground.

"On the bare ground, my head bathed by the blithe air, and uplifted into infinite space, all mean egotism vanishes." That's Emerson in the process of having a transcendental moment. Maybe for a few minutes out there, some of us drank from the same ladle dipped in the same well.

The airplane went to work on the inside of the shimmering oval. It drew something like a pupil in the giant eye. This took time. It was done meticulously, as we continued to sleepwalk through our drills, ghost dancing with one another on the line. The defensive linemen let us block them, stepping with us almost gracefully, as though we were waltzing. Whenever possible we looked above. Soon it was nearly done. From the bottom of the circle, three roads converged on one spot, then one road headed up to the top of the circle. The eye stared down upon us.

Jonesy, our one bona fide hitter senior year, the heir of Paul and the Brain, identified it first. He did so peremptorily, and in the silent idiom of the great signifier above. He thrust a fist in the air, middle finger held erect: the American pledge of anti-allegiance. "Fuck you!" he bellowed.

The spell snapped. The pristine moment was done; Emerson's ladle got knocked to the ground; someone finally rolled up a magazine and smacked the bee out of the air. From every side you heard what sounded like a volley of rifle fire. Fuck you! Fuck you! Our cohort had been ambushed. We'd been taken by surprise by a subtle enemy.

It was clear to all that the emblem floating above wasn't some ad man's dream or a sky-borne joke. It was, in 1969, about the most provoking emblem you could produce: the peace sign. Most of my fellow football players greeted it with what you'd expect: loathing. Most of the Mustangs on the field that day acted their part, a part they shared with construction workers and policemen and firemen and factory laborers and the other people at the heart of what President Nixon would soon be calling the silent majority. Most of my fellow ballplayers did exactly what you'd expect them to do. Most did, but not all.

In 1969 the Vietnam War was burning away as it would be for the next four years and more. We were kids—sixteen, seventeen, eighteen—and we were ripe to be drafted as soon as we graduated. Many of us would be prospects for the army and the Marines. (The navy and the air force were for rich kids.) The diversions that being a senior in high school brings can often blot out thoughts about the future. But for us, in 1969, this was not true. I was getting phone calls from military recruiters; almost all of us were. We all knew guys who had been to Vietnam; we knew guys who had come back badly wounded or damaged in spirit; we all knew of guys who had not come back, period. The prospect of execution does wonders to concentrate the mind, Samuel Johnson said. We weren't looking at execution, not exactly. But our prospects at the time couldn't help but encourage us to think.

It was plain to us Mustangs that we had been getting a form of premilitary training there on the practice field behind the Hormel Stadium bleachers. At the beginning of our sessions we lined up in rows, much like soldiers, and we did our Alabama Quick Cals. At a signal, we thrust our right forearms out and hollered, "Beat!" We retracted the right forearm, then thrust foreword the left, calling out the name of the team we'd be playing that week. Beat Somerville! Beat Malden! Beat Everett! Beat Revere! Then we went on to a sequence of other brisk movements with accompanying chants. We jerked our bodies in robotic sync. Sometimes we excised "Beat" and replace it with "Kill!" Kill Somerville! Kill Malden! Kill Everett! The assistant coaches nodded approval.

At the end of practice we lined up for the feared grass drills. There was chanting and hollering and whooping: signs of an attempt to take joy in the suffering as we shot our legs out from under us and pancaked on our bellies with a whop. The soldier suffered the rigors of conditioning for his country; we suffered for our team and our school. But we knew that what we were undergoing on the field was modeled on what was happening in South Carolina at Parris Island and at Fort Benning, in Georgia, where Marines and soldiers were grunting their way through basic training.

The early practices—the double sessions in particular, where I'd earned my uniform and begun to develop some football-style character—had a boot camp feel. Much like the Marine recruits in basic training, we were struggling to make it. None of us wanted to "wash out," though about a third did—roughly the quotient that washes out at Parris Island, I understand. You had to be rough and tough and you had to be determined to make it. All the time we were doing our drills and reeling in the heat and praying for water, the coaches were letting us know, sometimes subtly, sometimes not, that we were preparing to become soldiers.

The coach who instilled this warrior ideal most deeply was our junior year backfield coach, Joe Nutley. Nutley had been a Marine, been to Vietnam, and—word had it—been badly wounded: shrapnel in his back and his thigh. He had clearly modeled his coaching persona on a Marine drill instructor's. He was constantly getting up into our helmets and bawling commands. He roared at a million decibels. His philosophy of football was based not on strategy and technique, but on hustle, which he referred to as "huss." When we showed huss he commended us vehemently; when we pushed the needle into extra huss he was capable of ecstasy. "Atta boy! Atta boy!" To Nutley the game was about conditioning, attitude, effort, and desire: huss and extra huss.

And it was all about the team—just as, when he was in the Marines, it had been all about the Corps. On Nutley's football team there were no individuals; there was only the group. Kelly, the linebacker coach, was a thoroughbred, and he loved talent (which means he didn't much care for me). He'd say a word about team from time to time, but he held himself like an aristocrat who believed in the hegemony of the best. Not Nutley. On his football team—as in his Marines—there were no individuals. You won by forming a tightly disciplined unit of guys who sweated and strove together and, in a pinch, would do anything for each other. This is how Marines were surviving in Vietnam and had been surviving since the beginning of the Corps—all for one, one for all: the group before everything. Nutley never had to come out and directly state the association between his football team and his Marines: We all understood. It was part of what we were learning as Medford Mustangs. It was part of our education by football.

Football players are supposed to be warriors, and if they participate in a military mind-set without thinking too much about it, it's not surprising. So it made sense for Jonesy and Mike De Maria and Robbie Stang (who would soon be a Marine sergeant in Vietnam) to give the airborne peace sign the finger. It made sense for most of the team to holler invective back at the insult in the sky.

But there was more to it than that. It wasn't only that some of us didn't join in the derision, said nothing, and made no gestures. (That was me, of course: "both in and out of the game and watching and wondering at it.") But a few guys did something else entirely.

From Fred Chivakos and Rick Strong came a different greeting: hands raised, index and middle fingers spread. V for victory. But more than that: V for peace. Jimmy Jensen, the only black kid on the team, thrust his hand up too, or I believe he did. (I'm not sure.) The coaches stared in surprise bordering on shock. Jonesy and his pals looked with pure contempt at the two (or three) reprobates.

This was Medford (pronounced "Meffa"), a working-class town, conservative and Catholic. And these three (let's say three) guys were ballplayers—all could deliver the body-slamming news. They weren't cowards or shirkers. But they thought what they thought, and that was that. The players reminded me of the African American athletes who raised their black-gloved fists on the medal stand in Mexico City in 1968. (My father had come out strong on their behalf.) That gesture went round the world, of course. But in the small world of Mustang ball, this sudden gesture had its resonance too.

The guys were the first people I knew outside my family who made a noise against the war. (My father had registered a protest early, but his view shifted as time passed.) Those peace signs my buddies thrust up into the sky, with the giant inspiration in the background—to others they might not have been much. For my money, they were something to see.

What were they doing with that act of defiance? What did it

mean for a few high school football players to come out against the war? One thing they did was to get a debate going. From then on there was give-and-take in the locker room about Vietnam. It may not have been the most intelligent or best-informed discussion that you'd hear on the subject. None of us would be asked to appear on public television to debate Robert McNamara or help bolster his position. But we did begin to talk candidly among ourselves about how we viewed the fighting. No one was shouted down. No one was humiliated. The talk could get passionate, and you wouldn't always call it polite, but it was enriching talk. And outside that class with my brilliant philosophy teacher, the Mustang locker room was the only place I knew of where you could find it.

Those three guys got a conversation started about football and war that had strong bearing for us all at the time. They got me thinking. They probably got the whole team doing that. And the thoughts that started that day on the field early in my football education have continued for me through time.

It's no news that football values and military values appear to fuse seamlessly. Football is as close to war as a game can be without sliding over into war pure and simple. There's something military about the life of the football player. The process of trying out and making it through practice and getting a place on the team is a direct reflection of military basic training. Devotion to team, responsiveness to coaches, commitment to discipline and duty—those values have a military resonance. So it's not surprising to go to a football game and see that the marching band is a military band and that a color guard representing all the services stands at the fifty-yard line while the national anthem plays. It's no shock that they unfold a massive American flag at halftime and that navy jets streak overhead. It makes sense that the military and naval academies will face off every year on live TV not on a soccer field or across chessboards, but in a football stadium. Football is a military game; football is a patriotic game. What more is there to say?

Maybe there is something. Football resembles war, but what kind of war, exactly?

Football resembles the kind of war in which you can see your opponent and grapple with him one-to-one. Of course, there's a technology at play in football. You have to aim the ball; you have to throw it, the way you would a missile. But most of the combat in football is hand-to-hand. You look into your opponent's eyes through his face mask, and he looks into yours. You match strength to strength. Football evokes war, yes. But football evokes a war in which you can readily view your opponent and go at him directly. Football smacks of the kind of combat that took place in the American Civil War, or in the struggles between the U.S. Cavalry and the Indian tribes.

Football also evokes a war that's fair. You can spring surprises, you can import trick plays, but each side plays by the same rules. Both put eleven men on the field; all players on the team wear the same-color jerseys; no team has special material advantages, like the ability to launch the ball mechanically down the field rather than throwing it. There is some home-field edge, but no team comes to the game with a radical material advantage over the other.

How different is the kind of war that football evokes from the wars that America fights in the present and probably will continue to fight? How different is football from the Vietnam War that my buddies and I were preparing for on the field the day that peace sign materialized and from the kinds of wars that America now fights all over the world? Our current wars are anything but personal and immediate. Men kill each other from vast distances. They fly over in planes and drop bombs; they send drones out to destroy human targets. Or, on the other side of the equation, they create their own bombs out of scrap and place them along much-traveled roads: improvised antipersonnel devices. There is occasionally physical contact in current warfare. Soldiers and Marines do sometimes see and grapple with their enemies.

There were pitched battles in the Vietnam War. In the Tet Offensive, the Vietcong managed to infiltrate Saigon and launch a surprise attack. And when the Americans fought back, the VC did not run, as they usually did. (This willingness to fight American troops head-to-head virtually destroyed the Vietcong.) In the Battle of Najaf, in Iraq in 2004, the Marines squared off against the Mahdi Army, fighting them at close quarters from one tomb to the next in the Najaf cemetery. (The Mahdi Army had about the same luck against American Marines as the Vietcong did at Tet.) But neither of these battles is representative of what U.S. forces have done over the past fifty years. Physical strength and daring still do sometimes matter in war. But frequently war is fought from afar. An American sniper now often carries a rifle that can kill a foe who is as much as a mile away.

There are no jerseys; there are no clearly demarcated teams. The enemy is surely the sniper aiming down from a minaret. But it may also be the middle-aged woman approaching a checkpoint, wearing a belt packed with TNT and ball bearings. Nor is current war in any sense fair. The prevalent American strategy is to crush the enemy with massive and overwhelming force. The insurgent strategy is surprise, deception, and ambush. Roughly equal sides no longer face each other across a no-man's-land; there are no more cavalry charges; the hand-to-hand encounter that defined military action from Homer as far up as, perhaps, the First World War still exists, but it is not central to most victories and defeats.

Football approximates war? Yes, true enough. But it helps to be more exact. The training for football is a lot like military training—it's solid preparation for boot camp. The coach's football ideology is close to military ideology. It's all about the team; all for one, one for all: Commit yourself to ideals that are larger than yourself. (It's said that on his deathbed, Vince Lombardi cried out, "Joe Namath, you're not half as big as you think you are. You're not bigger than football, Joe Namath. Oh, no, you're not!"—or something like that.) *Preparation* for the game has a military dimension, no doubt about it.

And the game itself has all sorts of martial associations too. George Carlin got it right. But the kind of war that football evokes—personal, immediate, hand-to-hand, and fair—is a kind of war that doesn't get fought anymore. It's war in the nineteenth-century style that football evokes (if that), not present-day war. We simply don't fight that way now. A young man could think that education by football would be good preparation for what he'd see in a modern war, but he'd be sadly mistaken. For football is not a reflection of modern war. It is an *idealization* of war.

My buddies and I working out behind the stands at Hormel Stadium were being educated to think that we were much like soldiers, and that practice was training and the games were akin to combat. Practice *is* like training. Yet some of us thought that the games were combat and joined the Marines and the army with this idea in the back of their heads (or in the front). The Vietnam War was nothing like a football game. And the wars in Iraq and Afghanistan are even less like what goes on at Soldier Field and War Memorial Stadium than Vietnam was.

Watching football on TV and at the stadium can blur your sense of the relationship between the game and the military too. On American TV football and the military are in a symbiotic relationship, with soldiers on the sidelines and the color guard parading on the field. The NFL is happy to accept all the military affiliation it can get and the army is happy to be connected to sports. But the result can be, especially for the young, a dose of miseducation through football. Football looks more heroic than it is and the army looks more glamorous than it could ever be.

Football players aren't heroes the way soldiers who risk their lives every day are, but the association between the military and the football industry can make you believe so. The NFL is in the star-creation business, for a number of reasons. The military association helps with the creation of stars. Being a soldier is not a glamorous job—but young men and women often need to believe that it is, in order to join up. The association between high-paid, high-living athletes and the armed services lends allure to soldiering. The army confers the heroic aura and picks up some glamour; football lends glamour and gets some Homeric glory for itself.

The perception that the novelist Ben Fountain confers on his protagonist in *Billy Lynn's Long Halftime Walk* rings true. "Why, please, do they play the national anthem before games anyway? The Dallas Cowboys and the Chicago Bears, these are two privately owned, for-profit corporations, these their contractual employees taking the field. As well play the national anthem at the top of every commercial, before every board meeting, with every deposit and withdrawal you make at the bank."

My buddies on that practice field, holding up the peace sign, were maybe beginning to see that football wasn't war and war wasn't football. They were all good ballplayers. Yet they showed that to be a good ballplayer, you didn't have to buy the military mind-set.

Americans like to think of athletes as heroes. The average fan can name at least two dozen NFL players that he worships, two dozen at least. They are the members of his sports pantheon, his gods. But how many heroes from Iraq and Afghanistan can he name? How many will he be able to name in the wars to come? Unless he is a fighter himself, or has close friends or family in the military, the answer is predictable. The answer is zero. War now is confusing and it has been for some time. Many people do not know whether our wars in the Middle East have been good or bad, right or wrong. Should we be there? Should we withdraw? War is also a cause of some guilt. Why do almost exclusively poor kids go? Why is there no draft? Why are we in wars that have not been officially declared? With all these concerns and anxieties, does it really make sense to call the fighters who have gone to the Middle East heroes, to chronicle their achievements and to celebrate them?

These are hard questions, not readily answered. It is much easier to turn away from the issue of current-day military heroism and find martial heroes in the game of football. Football is not war, but it is enough like war (we feel) to be a good substitute. By thinking about football and not war, by thinking about football heroes and not war heroes, jocks and not Marines, people are able to turn away from the difficulties that political life presents and trade them in for simplicity. Few people savor complexity. Few people wish to be in uncertainties, mysteries and doubts, to use the poet's words. Football does many things. But one thing it does is to transfer our attention from hard ethical and political issues to clearer and simpler ones.

Sports are an irony-free zone—maybe the only irony-free zone in our culture. Talking about sports, people can use terms like *raw courage* and *dedication* and *loyalty* without inflecting them with doubt. Can you talk about raw courage in a war that people don't understand and maybe don't approve of? You generally can't. Generally you have to register some form of reservation when you praise a soldier now. The war might be unjust. We might learn that the "hero's" deeds were misrepresented to the public. So we transfer our hunger for heroism away from the area where real heroism has traditionally been possible and relocate it to the less complex realms of sport.

When the New York Giants won the 2012 Super Bowl, the city of New York turned out and gave them a ticker-tape parade through the canyons of Wall Street. Everyone in New York loved it—almost. A number of Iraq War veterans stepped forward and asked the obvious question. What about us? When is our parade? When, they asked implicitly, will you celebrate heroes who truly are heroes? When will you step away from simulation and deal with the real thing?

October 15, the day we saw the peace sign in the sky, was a special day. It was a day devoted to mobilizing all the forces in America that were against the war in Vietnam. There were demonstrations across the country. The peace sign that appeared that day was designed chiefly for a crowd about ten miles away on the Boston Common. There were a hundred thousand people there to protest the war and to listen to George McGovern and others speak against it.

Not much later there would be another antiwar rally on the Common, and a few Mustang ballplayers (Fred Chivakos among them) would turn up to hear speakers like Abbie Hoffman. Hoffman was a founder of the yippies, the Youth International Party, a gang of hippies who had gone the anarchist route. He once said that he was happy to protest the Vietnam War and American imperialism and all the rest. But his main gripe against the government was that it didn't let him and his friends get together on their own piece of land, smoke a lot of weed, fornicate freely, make noise, and generally do what they pleased. Abbie supposedly said that America was trying to defeat a people— the North Vietnamese—made invincible by their devotion to the collective doctrine, communism. He said that North Vietnamese babies were pulling American fighter planes out of the sky with their bare hands and dashing them on the ground. He got pretty carried away with himself.

A lot of people did at the time. And the passions of those antiwar people made their way to the Hormel Stadium practice field. The peace sign in the sky—which Jonesy said looked like the footprint of the great American chicken—touched us. Three guys showed it recognition. They responded in kind. And from then on the football team was different. There was talk about the war. Positions were respected. No one got shouted away. Arguments that were crude and clublike got refined.

This was Medford—Meffa. Everybody was patriotic, everybody was for the government: my country right or wrong, and all that. But not these guys, and in a while not me, either. By the end of the year there were at least five or six of us football players— dumb jocks—with a word to say against the war and often more than that. Who was right? Who was wrong? Those questions matter, sure. But it matters too that young kids were starting to think for themselves—and once people start doing that, they don't always stop.

What gave those three guys the wherewithal to part company with the group and get a debate rolling? It's impossible to say for sure. On some level human motivations can't be plumbed. But I believe that part of their courage came from what football had given them. They were surer of themselves than they would have been if they hadn't managed to negotiate double sessions (twice) and do all those up-downs and face Paul and the Brain across the line. You walked with more confidence when you could do that, and you talked with a little more too.

Those guys who flashed the peace sign conformed to many of the mores of the game. They played hard, hit hard. But they bucked some of the game's military values too—and it was the game, I believe, that allowed them to do it. I think that they used what their football education had taught them to rebel against the duller, dimmer side of football.

As for me, what the guys did that day got me thinking. I was getting calls from the Marine Corps recruiter. And I was open to signing up. But after that day I began to ponder the war and whether it was just or unjust, good or bad. In time, I'd be looking into books on Vietnam and reading the newspapers every day to try to figure the situation out. (Up until then, I'd only read the sports page.) It took a while, but those guys woke me up—those guys instilled with the confidence that football had given them to try to go their own ways. My education by football was having some effects—and some good ones. But they probably weren't quite the effects that Coach Nutley, sounding his Marine Corps yawp at us across that barren practice field, had in mind.

And they weren't quite the effects that my father might have hoped for, either. It was two years now since my sister's death, and my father was starting to right himself. That means he began keeping it to three nights out playing cards and drinking and that he returned to sleep in his own bed (for at least two hours) nearly every night. He and I watched football from time to time, but now, on the nights he was home, we also sat together to watch Johnny Carson's show. My father adored Carson; he loved the way Johnny dealt with all his big-shot guests. Carson was amiable, interested, but only up to a point. No movie star or entertainer, no big-name author ever got to pontificate or preen on Johnny's show. He lowered his head, cocked it sideways, and gave the skeptical, kindly, killing Carson wink. Or he turned to Ed McMahon, yes-man of all time, and said, without speaking a word: How do I put up with this? How does anyone? Johnny was the late-night rep for my father and all the other little guys curious enough to want to see who was glowing bright in the American pantheon of the moment but determined not to worship anybody—unless, of course, it was Johnny.

Johnny listened and Johnny talked and so naturally, in the commercials and sometimes outside them, my father and I talked too. And what my father heard, he sometimes didn't like. I questioned the culture—the nine-to-five and the steady paycheck; I questioned President Nixon, whom my father had come to admire; I questioned America; and of course I questioned the war. My father tried to be like Johnny—to be skeptical and funny and urbane. But he couldn't always pull it off. He detonated at me and my new free-thinking ways more than once, though he always regretted it quickly. He blamed my behavior on the new philosophy course I was taking and a few times he threatened to come into school and set Franklin Lears right. (My father was joking—I think.) He blamed my mouthing off on the class where we read Plato and Freud, and from time to time he even blamed my behavior on himself—he had, after all, roamed the apartment when I was small, singing the Groucho Marx ditty that features the chorus "Whatever it is I'm against it." He was part right about both these influences, no doubt. My father wasn't a god to me anymore, though I still cared about what he believed. And Frank Lears was opening the world of thought to me and to my classmates. What my father failed to imagine was that my insubordination had another source—the football field. He couldn't see that in a strange way of my own, I was becoming more and more a football player.

6

A PUNCH AND A PRAYER: FAITH

We prayed before every game, gentle prayer, presided over by the head coach. We prayed for a fair contest; we prayed we would escape serious injury and that the other team would too. We prayed that we would emerge with a victory, if we were deserving.

But in the locker room before our contest with Everett, we got another kind of homily. It came from one of our assistant coaches, Coach Pelligrino, who taught not at Medford but at Everett High School, our opponent. He spent his days in the camp of the enemy. And all week, the Everett players and the coaches (dammit, the coaches!) had been stepping up to our man and telling him exactly what they were going to do to his team come Saturday. By game time, Coach Pelligrino, who was in charge of the tackles and ends, was in a state. And just before we went out onto the field against Everett—and just after our prayers—Coach Pelligrino let us know about it.

Then at halftime he really let fly. He preached a sermon that none of us Mustangs would forget. He showed us something about football and faith and even (dare one say it?) about America. He gave us a major installment of football education—but only if you had eyes to see and ears to hear.

When we played Everett, we had dreams of going on to be Greater Boston League champs. We'd rolled over North Quincy the week before, the Saturday after we'd seen the peace sign in the sky. I'd made four tackles in a row that day, my best showing by far. (All right, if we're honest I made three. But my buddy, an injured teammate who was in the booth helping the PA announcer, told him that I'd made the fourth one, because he didn't care for Johnny Rocco, the middle guard, who actually had.) Now we were determined to go undefeated. When the 1967 team won the championship, they'd gotten a trip to Bermuda, where they had, according to reports, drunk record amounts of beer and even met a Bermudan girl or two. They'd been compelled to stand in downtown Medford, wearing their football team jackets, shaking tin cans, and collecting change to raise money for the trip—which would be fine with us. But to get to Bermuda, we were going to have to beat Everett.

Almost all of the schools we played were located in cities in decay. We played against Watertown and Revere and Chelsea and Malden and Everett, working-class towns whose infrastructures seemed to be coming apart. We'd been to Chelsea a few weeks before and it looked like a slum from end to end, but Everett (which I'd grown up close by) didn't look too good either.

From our team bus we saw dilapidated three-decker houses squeezed one beside the other like bad teeth; every third store seemed to be selling liquor; factories coughed multicolored smoke even on a Saturday morning. At the stadium, the concrete seats were decomposing; pieces of them were scattered around like giant crumbs. The Everett players we passed on the way into our locker room wore faded red uniforms and what appeared to be the old-fashioned leather helmets that we'd seen in pictures of Jim Thorpe and his teammates. They looked more like World War I aviator hats than modern football helmets. The visitor's locker room smelled like a swamp. On the walls we saw mold. It was rare for us Medford kids to find someone to look down our noses at—but here in Everett it seemed that we had.

Plus the Everett team stunk. They played to about the level of their uniforms, from what we'd been told. Everyone beat them; everyone romped; everyone looked to the Everett game as a week off. As we trooped into the locker room wearing our stylish Mustang blue and sporting helmets clearly not designed for Jim Thorpe all-American or the Red Baron, we noticed the Everett linemen off doing drills. There were about a dozen of them and they were fat and meltingly soft—they looked like ice cream sundaes. Their red helmets were the cherries on top. We laughed at them for a while, and then we went inside the locker room to get our final instructions and to pray.

The head coach went quickly over the game plan, then he indicated it was time for the team prayer. With a clattering of cleats and bumping of shoulder pads, we lowered ourselves down on our knees. Some of us went to one knee, the way we did when the coaches told us to take a blow on the field. But most got on both knees, as we did when we received Holy Communion at the altar rail. (We Mustangs, coaches included, were almost all Catholics. I used to see the head coach at Sunday mass with his three daughters, one of whom was plain, one pretty, and one ethereally beautiful. They seemed like a family out of a fairy tale.) The head coach's prayer was, as always, subdued. He prayed that no one in the game would get seriously hurt—not on our side and not on our opponent's side, either. He prayed that the game would be fair and that we would all uphold the standards of good sportsmanship. He asked Jesus Christ and the Lord God to bless us and our homes and our families. He asked the Lord to grant us a win if we were deserving.

The head coach said a gentle amen and up we rose. But our line coach, Coach Pelligrino, the guy who taught at Everett High, had something to add. As soon as the head coach's prayer was over, Coach Pelligrino stepped forward and addressed the troops.

He told us that he had just experienced the worst week of his life as a teacher in the Everett school system. He had been challenged. He had been mocked. A kid who weighed a hundred pounds had stood in the coach's airspace and informed him that he and his blue minions were in for slaughter; the Mustangs had no chance.

Usually, Coach Pelligrino was reasonably controlled, at least for a coach. From time to time he did take off his Mustang blue

baseball hat, throw it on the ground, and perform a fiery inter-
pretive dance around it. But we had to screw up pretty badly to
earn that. We liked Coach Pelligrino, who was short and amiably bearlike and usually kept himself pretty well in check. But it
was plain to see that this time, he was ready to burst and let flow.

"I wanted to punch that kid in the mouth," Coach Pelligrino
muttered half to himself and half to us. "I wanted to punch him
right in the mouth."

It grew silent. We all waited.

"Punch him right in the mouth!" This time it was louder and
echoed slightly off the green walls.

The head coach stepped in. "Amen," he said. "Amen."

Then we were clattering and bumping, bumping and clattering, and headed for the worn locker room door yelling about
hitting and victory and punching Everett in the mouth. Beside
me as we passed through the decaying door was Rick Strong,
who was in my philosophy class. He was one of the guys who had
shot the peace sign up when the spirit in the sky materialized.
"Do you really think," he asked me, "that Jesus gives a shit
whether we beat Everett or not?"

Religion is part of football. Players often kneel to pray before
a game, the way that we did. Afterward they thank God for the
victory or ask him to reconcile them to the loss. When someone goes down on the field, about a third of the players on both
teams sink to their knees and offer up a prayer for the guy's

well-being. At the end of games, there's frequently a prayer circle, where players gather to thank the Lord for whatever they might be feeling thankful for, their having survived the afternoon in one piece probably preeminent.

When a player breaks into the end zone on a run or grabs a touchdown pass, it's not uncommon for him to point a finger skyward: Thank you, Lord; I owe it all to you. (Clearly the guy never met Rick Strong.) Priests and ministers and rabbis don't march across the football field before the game, the way soldiers, sailors, and marines do, but religion is still there. In high school and college in particular, Jesus and the eternal Father preside over the contest.

We take this for granted. I surely did, at least until that day of the Everett game, when Rick asked me if I thought that Jesus cared one way or another who won. I'd really never thought much about the conjunction of football and faith and, when you really consider it, how strange the coupling is.

Football seems to us a conservative game; it makes sense that it mixes well with other emblems of American conservatism, like religion and the military. The most football-happy states in America tend to be the ones where religion reigns. Red states are all about first and ten and a banging defense; blue states, generally less so.

But is religion—and Christianity in particular—really compatible with the smashmouth values of football? You don't need to read the Gospels long to sense a contradiction. Jesus preaches forgiveness. It's not a momentary whim of his: The idea that you forgive trespassers against you is perhaps *the* central idea in Matthew, Mark, and Luke. (It's slightly less important in John.) When someone smites you on one cheek, what are you supposed to do? On this matter Jesus is not equivocal. You don't forgive a sinner once, the Savior says: You forgive him time after time—seven times seven, if need be. When Jesus comes upon a group of men eager to stone a woman to death for having committed adultery (they think), he speaks the famous words: "Let him who is without sin cast the first stone."

Jesus, whom so many worshippers of football also profess to worship, is born into two cultures: the culture of imperial Rome and the culture of the Jews. The Romans are a warrior culture—their ethos comes out of Homer; Julius Caesar seeks to emulate Achilles—and they are a successful one. The Jews are also a warrior culture—in his earliest manifestations, Yahweh is, among other things, a war god—and they are only intermittently successful. The Jews spend much of their history in defeat and servitude. Servitude is their condition when Jesus is born; they're under the Roman yoke, a mild one compared with others they have borne. But both cultures, Roman and Jewish, are warrior cultures. Jesus arrives with something new. Love your neighbor, he says. But don't merely love your neighbor—that's not terribly hard when you come down to it. Love your enemy too.

Jesus has almost nothing in common with the Romans, and he departs significantly from the Jewish tradition, at least on the matter of violence. He is much closer to the teachings of the Buddha and the wisdom of the Hindu Upanishads. Life is holy, they tell us. The human being is divine. Do no harm: Bring only peace and gentleness to all, for all are in need. Their lives are defined by suffering; their beings are full of pain. The last act that the Buddha performs is not unlike Jesus's last act. Gautama smilingly forgives the man who has fed him the tainted pork that will soon kill him. (Gautama has been tramping around India in the mud and the dust and the monsoons for forty years, preaching—he may not be entirely unhappy to be making an end.) Jesus blesses his killers. Lord forgive them, he says. They know not what they do.

About the angriest Jesus gets is when he picks up a whip and drives the moneylenders out of the temple. He picks it up—that's all. He never hits anyone with it. (There is the puzzling episode with the fig tree. He zaps it because . . . why? He zaps it because he does.) But Jesus, like the Buddha and like Confucius, preaches gentleness. Love the Lord your God with your whole heart and soul and mind. Love your neighbor as yourself.

In America every Sunday, Americans go off to church to worship Jesus. They take in his teachings. They hear the beautiful parable of the Samaritan. They learn how he pulls the beaten man out of the ditch and dresses his wounds and takes him to an inn and leaves his own purse to pay the expenses. Or in the week before Easter they listen to the story of Jesus telling the thief crucified on one side of him that he'll see the man that night in heaven, and they listen to him forgive his torturers. They take in the Gospel of forgiveness. Then they go home, turn on the television set, and watch young men try to bust each other's spleens.

I don't think we Mustangs broke any spleens after our prayers the day of the Everett game. But we did do some damage. All through the first half we ran them over. Those big linemen moved like men underwater. They had the slo-mo stride of elephants on parade. Our backs streaked around them. Coach Pelligrino ascended to heaven. He laughed to himself and maybe he talked to himself a little too. This was what he wanted. This was what the coach had prayed for.

But on the last play of the half something happened. We were up by a few touchdowns and feeling fat and happy and by now almost bemused at Everett and its pachyderm linemen and its fruit-fly backs. We punted to them. We gave up the ball. The guy who caught the punt probably had no business catching punts. He was short and squat as a fire hydrant and ran with a bowlegged stride. But he did run. He ran all over the field. He only sometimes ran in the direction of our goal line, though overall that was his trajectory. Mostly he ran so as not to get tackled. He slid to the Everett sideline and tried to turn upfield, but seeing his route blocked, he turned and headed for his own end zone. No dice. Now he was cutting back and heading to the other sideline—ours. No one could catch him, but I'm not sure anyone was trying that hard. He was like the clown who comes on at the rodeo to divert the bull and let the cowboy escape. This guy was clown pudgy and clown awkward, and in the absurd uniform with the flyboy hat he looked more like an entertainer than a ballplayer. He was the halftime show, early.

Still, no one could catch him. He was making football into a farce. He zipped by me where I was standing on the sidelines and he was gasping like a steam engine. I almost jabbed out my foot to trip him. His sins were so many—he'd ruined the aesthetic of the game, among other things—that I might actually have been forgiven. (After five or six years passed.) But I refrained and on he went. It seemed to continue for an hour, though it was probably something like twenty seconds, tops. The kid dodged over the field like a fly dodging over a pond full of trout—snap and miss, snap and miss, snap, miss. You almost thought that God was on *his* side. Not far from me, Coach Pelligrino threw his hat on the ground and stared at it as though contemplating a pissed-off pas de deux.

The stadium roared as the kid ran. It had been quiet until then except for our marching band and our small contingent of fans, but now the joint was rocking with the sounds of mock triumph. Maybe Everett couldn't beat us, but they could make us look ridiculous, and given how their season had gone so far, they'd take it. The Everett band began to play chaotic music as the kid ran; the tubas, of which there seemed to be about a dozen, sounded loudest, but there was plenty of percussion too. There rose above us The Chaotic Sonata for Tuba and Drum, improvised by the Everett High School marching band in honor of the humiliation of mighty unbeaten and untied Medford.

And then the runner stopped. He seemed to expire somewhere around midfield. He half-collapsed and a few blue jerseys collapsed on top of him. The half was over. We went back into the locker room and this time, contrary to custom, we prayed again.

But first we got to hear Coach Pelligrino really cut loose. His first installment had been tea and cakes. Now he was in hurricane mode. It was a well-constructed rant. He screamed invective at the Everett football team, then the Everett school system, then the city of Everett, and in between each segment there was a refrain: "I wanted to punch him in the mouth!" There was no hat dance; not enough space. But there was no strategizing; there was no reflection on whether we should blitz more or blitz less, pass long or pass short, run up the middle or around the end—no chalk talk. There was only the invective cut up into topics, and the refrain: "I wanted to punch him in the mouth." A thick fist traveled through the air. Spit flew. If the spit hit you—it didn't hit me—it would have been worth your life to make a show of brushing it off. Don't spray it! Say it! No one came forward with that grade-school mantra either.

"I wanted to punch him in the mouth!" It was as though the boiler in the basement had burst. It had been threatening to blow for a while, but now it actually popped. Kids often don't know what to do when adults lose it. ("Punch him in the mouth!") And it's particularly hard when a coach goes over the side: There's always the possibility that one will actually smack you—then what? We'd seen coach Pelligrino mad before. But this was different. This was wrath of another order. It was the anger of someone who had been badly humiliated and was now insisting on retribution and more retribution. The coach wanted payback. ("Punch him!") He wanted an eye for an eye. He wanted the destruction of the erring city of Everett. ("In the mouth!") His wrath was—why not say it?—his wrath was biblical.

Eventually Coach Pelligrino had to breathe. He was red and panting and if he didn't breathe he would expire. So he took a breath. And when he did the head coach stepped in with some simple words. "Let us pray," he said. And we did. We prayed that the game would unfold fairly, that no one would be hurt, and that if we deserved to win, we would. Then we headed back onto the field.

In our culture it seems that it is often the most devoted Christians—the ones who claim to love Jesus in the loudest voices—who are most attached to the Saturday and Sunday spleen bustings. How can this be? Are people in general (and Americans in particular) so blind that they can merrily hold two contradictory beliefs together in their minds and hearts and not be bothered? Perhaps we're all just eager to have our pious commitments and our violent diversions. Maybe we're like little kids who desperately want to have their cake and eat it too. But we're better than little kids in that we've found out how to accomplish it. You just do it! You worship Jesus and you worship the forearm shiver and to hell with anyone who doesn't like it.

But maybe matters are more complicated. It pays to recall occasionally that the majority of Americans are not Christian per se; we do not simply follow the teachings of the Galilean. We follow the Gospels and we follow the Old Testament. And those, as a long line of renegade teachers, starting at least with Marcius and moving through William Blake and Arthur Schopenhauer have taught, are rather different kinds of texts.

To put it crudely: There's nothing pacifist about the Yahweh of the Hebrew Bible. He has nothing to say about turning the other cheek or about forgiving anyone seven times seven. Yahweh drowns nearly the whole world when he gets exasperated at its sinful ways; he destroys Sodom and Gomorrah in a blink; He murders the firstborn of the Egyptians; he drowns Pharaoh's army under the roiling Red Sea.

Yahweh is also the creator god, of course. Out of his love He makes the heavens and the earth, the seas and the stars. He gives life to Adam by taking up a handful of red clay and breathing into it. His connection with His creatures, especially those He favors, is strong and deeply loving. He is a generous and watchful Father to his people.

But He can also be a wrathful figure who makes violent demands. When King Saul conquers the Amalekites, the Lord tells him that he must kill every living being: man, woman, child, all the way down to the livestock. Saul spares a handful of them, no more. The Lord becomes so enraged with him that He decrees Saul's kingship must come to an end. The prophet Samuel nearly kills Saul in God's name. As the Bible unfolds, Yahweh seems to become less vengeful and more humane. The prophets Isaiah and Jeremiah beseech Him to care for the poor and the widows, and sometimes he no doubt listens.

Jews in America seem to have evolved away from allegiance to a God of vengeance. Many have contributed in distinguished ways to a culture that is worldly and tolerant and based in a commitment to justice. It is, oddly, Christians who seem most inclined to hang on to the vision of the God of judgment who presides in the sky and takes hard vengeance on his enemies. Many American Christians worship this God and they worship the God of peace and love: Jesus Christ, born of the Virgin Mary.

We Americans like to have our cake and eat it too. We like to believe that we are kind and charitable and generous—true followers of Jesus. And often we are. When there is flood or famine in the world, we're there, quickly and with great resources. When someone's down, we try to pull him up. But we also want to be able to slip into another mode. We want to be able to take revenge, ruin our enemies. We want to judge our rivals in the balance and find them wanting, to take a famous phrase from the Book of Daniel. We want triumph and domination. Our nation's major religion, as it's structured, gives us the freedom—if you want to call it that—to slip from one way of being to the other, and to do so with justification, religious justification. When we seek victory we are acting in one well-sanctified mode; when we seek peace and offer (or ask for) forgiveness, we act in another, equally sanctified. When we praise Jesus and then go home to watch the football wars, we are enjoying the fruits of a paradox that we've exploited for a long time. Rick, my freethinking football educator, may have sensed something like this the day we were spilling out of the foul-smelling Everett locker room. It took me a while longer to catch on.

My mother would not have spoken a word against what the coach said that day—my mother never spoke a word against anyone in authority. In matters of faith, she listened to the priest and that was that. But during her trial after my sister's death, it was to the suffering and forgiving Jesus that she turned. When she lit candles in the basement of the church, she prayed to Jesus that he would help to bear her sufferings, as he had borne his own. She had no interest in a punitive, vindictive, all-conquering sky god. It was the example of Jesus, along with the love of her mother and sister, that in time pulled her up from despair and pulled her through.

I'll bet the Everett players heard the speech about the punch in the mouth through the decrepit walls that separated the teams. It might have whipped them up—if they needed any more whipping up after the carnival run before halftime. The run proved to be irrelevant, but also decisive. Irrelevant: The kid didn't score. But it inspired the Everett squad. When they came out of their locker room onto the field it sounded like a far squat of hell had been granted weekend furlough. "Shut that door!" the head coach hollered. The sound was shaking our walls. "It *is* shut!" a lineman buddy of mine yelled back.

The game began again. Suddenly Everett's elephant linemen were executing controlled stampedes and running us down; their fruit-fly backs were un-swattable. Now Everett's Jim Thorpe helmets didn't look like sorry relics; they looked like tokens of a purer football past. Their ratty stadium felt like a venerable monument. Suddenly they were kicking the shit out of us. All our prayers (and our coach's rants) seemed to be in vain.

The game was like being in a bad dream—or if you were me, it was like watching a bad dream from the sidelines. We fumbled, they grabbed it; our Namath-like slinger tossed a wobbly pass, they picked it off; their line pulled left and our linebackers followed them, leaving their quarterback isolated on the right. (Good-bye.) On offense we couldn't move the ball; on defense we couldn't stop them.

What had happened? They were inspired by the crazy-legs run, sure. And no doubt our coach's well-structured clubhouse rant had inspired them too. ("Punch him in the mouth!") They were losing and probably finished at the half, despite the run. But if our coach could get that cranked up about the game—hey, maybe there was still hope.

Or maybe we got ourselves confused.

Is it possible that the head coach and the line coach put us in a tailspin? One was about playing fair and not getting hurt and being good sports and respecting the other team. The other was about punching guys in the mouth. There it was if you wanted to see it—the Gospels and a salient dimension of the Old Book colliding. Coach Pelligrino was all about wrath and destruction;

the head coach was the prophet of fairness and light. But I doubt the collision really had much to do with our loss to Everett. It was weird what we were hearing, no doubt: Be fair, be humane, treat your opponent with respect. But on the other hand: Be strong, be brutal, win at all costs. (Be a football player!)

Still, I doubt we lost the game that day because we were confused by a contradiction. We lost because . . . we lost because Everett scored more points than we did. But the Everett game highlighted something important about an education by football. The day concentrated an American dilemma, difficult for any kid to negotiate. The world was telling us to be kind and the world was telling us to be hard, to hit or be hit. Which was it? How should I really behave? How should I act, not only here on the field but out in my life at large? There's much to be learned from the Hebrew Bible and the Gospels, both. But when you try to force them together, you're creating the basis for serious confusion. Justice or mercy? The law or the forgiveness of sins?

It would be too much to ask a football education to untangle big cultural contradictions. That activity is for another branch of schooling. But the marriage of football and religion makes a confusing situation yet more confusing, especially for someone who is young—though Rick seemed to grasp the point right away. Does Jesus *really* care if we beat Everett? I'm guessing (though who can know?) that Jesus, teacher of gentleness and forgiver of sins, may not even care who's going to take the Super Bowl this year.

7

THAT BLACK KID: MANLINESS

Malden, the team that we went up against in my last high school football game, had a black star. His name was Johnny Joy and he played defensive back and returned punts. In the week and a half leading up to the game, one of our assistant coaches got mildly obsessed with Johnny. He didn't talk about Johnny all the time— far from it. But when he did, he could get a little out of control: You imagined a car slip-sliding on an icy country road. "Johnny Joy," the coach chanted. "Johnny—the Boy—Joy." He'd drop into what he clearly thought was black inflection. "He gonna kick your butts, fellas. Johnny Joy. Johnny the Boy!" Sometimes it became a kind of show tune, performed in blackface. "Johnny Joy! Johnny the Boy!" The coach was hyperwhite, a screaming-skull motivator. But when he tried to get our spirits up to fight our rivals, he became a white man speaking black speak to mock a black kid.

The game was the last time that many of us would wear

Mustang blue. For almost all of us seniors, it was the last time that we'd play a game of full-out tackle football with pads and helmets. (Only one of the Medford seniors I knew of went on to play on a college team, and he was, like me, a reserve lineman who rarely got into the games. He played for Tufts and by all accounts played well.) Most of us felt that this game would be our last.

We wanted some redemption. After the Everett game the season hadn't gone well: Everett had broken our four-game unbeaten streak and then we'd been clubbed by Newton (beaten by rich kids!) and knocked around badly by Quincy on the coldest, hardest field I'd ever played on. I tried to tackle a tight end, a guy who outweighed me by thirty pounds, and when I bounced off him and hit the frozen ground, I felt all the fillings in my teeth jump. I thought my back was broken, but from our bench I heard one of the coaches holler, "Get up and walk it off! You're OK." I did and was.

Our team managed to beat Revere, a tough squad that dedicated the game to the memory of one of its players, who had died a few days before. (There seemed something cruel about winning that one.) We had five wins and three losses going into the final contest—at best a so-so season, given our early hopes. But a win against Malden could make up for a lot.

The game has some history to it. The Medford-Malden contest is the second-oldest continuous high school rivalry in the nation, started in 1889. It's played on Thanksgiving morning, one year in Malden, the next, Medford. My final year in the game

was a Medford year. The stadium always filled for it. Local people who never watched a football game came out for Medford-
Malden before they went home to carve their turkeys and watch
the pros on TV. Graduates of the two schools came back, especially former ballplayers. We knew that the stands would be full
of one-time Medford Mustangs, including members of the Nine
and 0 squad of 1967. We pronounced the names of those guys as
though they were names of the saints.

Malden was good that year. They'd lost a game or two early,
but by the end of the season they were probably the best team in
the league—maybe (as our head coach admitted) the best team
in the state. They had a Mack truck fullback and a stomping
defense that included Johnny Joy and a fast, smart middle guard.
(I'd known a lot of the kids on the team when I lived in Malden.)
Our head coach dryly informed us that their pass-rushing defensive end (whom I'd known in junior high as a heartthrob who
refused to cut his long blond hair when the assistant principal
issued orders) had sacked opposing quarterbacks more often than
our entire defensive line. By the end of the year the Malden players were body-slamming their opponents. We had our star quarterback, the Namath-style slinger who could also run, and Coach
Wilson was capable of a shrewd game plan, dryly dispensed, of
course.

The weekend before the game, Malden did us what seemed
like a favor. A bunch of their players (apparently) broke into
our stadium on Friday or Saturday night and spray-painted their
names all over the clubhouse wall. There was the name of their

stud fullback; the initials of the fast, smart middle guard; the carefully scripted name of their slightly shaky quarterback. And there in flamboyant script was the signature of their black star, Johnny Joy. The coaches lined us up and got us to walk past the scene as though we were novitiates getting our first look at a chapel desecrated by heathens.

It had the predictable effect. We were humiliated, enraged, and resolved to win no matter what. Our assistant coach went from mildly obsessed with Johnny to more than mildly. Johnny Joy. You all see what Johnny do? You see what Johnny think of you boys? What you gonna do to Johnny? What you gonna tell Johnny come Thursday? The coach wasn't always in this register. He could cut away and take a different angle. "You boys lose the game on Thursday," he told us (and told us), "your turkey is gonna taste like a baloney sandwich."

The coach was the motivator for this game, much as Coach Pelligrino had been for the Everett debacle, and the subject of his sermon was often, though not always, Johnny Joy. It was us against Johnny—us white guys out to redeem our dignity and (you couldn't say it but there it was) the dignity of our race against the black stud who dared even more dramatically than his teammates to desecrate the sanctum.

How did I respond to the coach's riffs? Probably not in any simple way, as an event that took place about a year before the Malden game suggests.

My junior year, I'd joined the track team after football was over, intent on being a shot-putter. I was surprisingly good, or at least not bad, at it. Shot putting is all about one powerful motion that you can rehearse a few million times if you're disposed. I was disposed (naturally) and got to the point where I could out-toss all but one of my fellow Mustangs and quite a few of our rivals. But shot putting didn't take much time, really, and I wanted to stay in shape. So I did some running, working hard on the quarter mile. When I first got interested in running the 440 I asked the coach what the strategy for the race was. He looked at me with genial puzzlement—he was a collegiate guy and had gone to Tufts or Villanova or something. "There is no strategy," he said. "You mean you just go all out all the way?" I asked. He nodded. If you have to ask a question about strategy for the quarter mile, you probably won't be much of a quarter miler.

But one meet there was what they called a "novice 440," a race for guys on the track team who . . . well, a race for guys on the track team who couldn't really run. There were a dozen of us out there that day, two each from the schools participating in the meet. One of us, a scrawny kid from Chelsea, was black. He was the runner I was determined to beat. On the last turn, I mustered a decent kick and caught up to him, then rambled to the finish line a few strides ahead—ahead of the black kid, that is; I placed somewhere in the middle of the pack.

My buddy Stan, who had been training me for the race, met me at the end. "One real push anywhere and you would have won," he told me. I acknowledged that this was so. "But," I said, "at least I beat the Negro"—but *Negro* was not the word I used. I was ashamed of myself for saying what I did and I could see that

Stan was surprised. This wasn't my usual way of talking, and Stan and I both knew it.

But it was my neighborhood idiom, for certain—it was the idiom of my old neighborhood in Malden, where other kids' dads had been willing to insult Jim Brown for the high crime of being black (though they did it from the safety of the far side of their television screens), and it was the idiom of my new city, Medford. This was 1969 and working-class guys around Boston—Irish and Italian and Polish—decent as they may have been in multiple ways, were likely to be racist at least to some degree. They weren't disposed to join the Klan (assuming there'd been a chapter around to join)—far from it—but the prevailing attitude toward blacks usually ran from mild suspicion to outright hostility.

In my own family it was different. My father had his flaws. (You could have asked my mother about them, if you had some time at your disposal.) But he was a thoroughly decent guy who had a welcoming attitude toward other people, whatever color or religion, especially if they were in the mood for a beer or a game of cards. I had a similar attitude, or thought I did, which was why I was surprised at myself for saying what I had after that race.

I said it at a sports event—a place where white anxieties about blackness can jump out of easy control. We white kids half-thought and fully feared that any black kid could beat us at any sport whatsoever. They'd show up our inferiority as men, or men in the making; they'd put us in our place. So how did I respond to Coach's riffs about Johnny? I'd guess I found them off-putting and distasteful, as my father would have; but I'm guessing that they may have gotten me a little juiced too. Who was the Malden team—and who was this Johnny Joy in particular, with his flashy signature—to defile our temple?

It isn't surprising that a coach and some of the rest of us got obsessed (mildly and then more than mildly) about a black star. With the exception of our one black player (and what was he thinking when our coach was doing his routines?) we were a white team. We were Italian and we were Irish with a few Polish kids thrown in, and we thought we were pretty tough. We believed that Medford had a football reputation (Greater Boston League champs 1967!) and we were determined to maintain it. But the prospect of playing against standout black players, or even one of them, was fraught for us. It was that way for almost all white players then, and over time it has probably gotten more so. In 1969, blacks were becoming more common on pro and upper-echelon college football teams. Now, though there are many fine white players in football, it isn't wrong to say that black players dominate both the pro and the high-level college game. Almost 70 percent of the players in the NFL today are black, though blacks make up only about 13 percent of our overall population. We probably felt this change coming on back there at Hormel Stadium in 1969 and were an adolescent combination of unhappy, confused, indifferent, and jazzed (those black players were often great) about it.

When we thought about Johnny Joy after we'd seen him on

the films that the Malden coach had brought over, most of us probably felt some fear. We were afraid of being popped by him if we caught a ball in his zone. We were afraid of him blowing by us on a kick return, a punt return, or (worst of all) an interception. We were scared of being hurt; we were scared of being humiliated—and the humiliation was probably what we feared more. I had no trouble imagining Johnny shooting by my nearsighted overeager self on a return. I'd commit myself too early; I'd buy his fake and he'd leave me in the mud.

Every autumn Saturday and Sunday in American football, players do astonishing deeds. They jump and bound, leap and dodge, and run at eye-searing speed. They seem for a while as if they're more than human. Some of the players who perform these feats are white, but the majority of the most graceful, fast, and daring are black. The wide receiver goes up and up and seems to hang in the air, outside time and beyond gravity, as he waits for the ball to hit him in the numbers. The renowned ballet dancer Mikhail Baryshnikov said that the best dancers in the world played in the NBA. He could have added the NFL. Players in pro football constantly do physical deeds to make the best-trained dancer gasp, and most, though hardly all, of the ones who do are black.

Whatever challenges Baryshnikov may have faced, there was never anyone poised to wait until he hit his apex and then try to break his back. NFL receivers live with this danger for years.

And they make the beautiful move and they catch the ball and then, as they hear the applause, they take the hit. I think that Baryshnikov may have risen a little higher (proportionally) than the best NFL wide receivers, but he got only applause.

Imagine what it takes to catch a pass across the middle in the NFL. You get free on a crossing pattern and for a moment you are open and you know that the ball is on the way. You also know that the instant you touch the ball—not catch it, but touch it—you'll be hit by one or two human missiles. They want to dislodge the ball. They want to make you drop it. But they also wouldn't mind totaling you.

There are seventy thousand people in the stadium and about twenty million watching on TV. If you show fear they will all see it. If you pull in your arms to protect yourself—"alligator arms"—everyone will know. The commentators will play the scene repeatedly and it will be fodder for the nightly sports broadcast. (In your clubhouse during film study, your coaching staff's equivalent of my old friend Kelly will mock you mercilessly.) So you hang in and when the ball comes you make your leap and show the world an image of beauty and guts. You grab the ball and you take a pop and the crowd cheers.

And most of the time, if you're watching the NFL now, it's a black guy who's doing the amazing deed and taking the pop (and delivering it too). Most NFL wide receivers are black; almost all running backs are—as well as defensive backs. (It's not surprising now for an NFL defense to field nine, ten, or even eleven African American players.) Those are the guys who do most of the amazing deeds. White players do some too but—shoot me if you like—they do fewer and often don't look as good doing them. Is this because black players come from a culture that values grace and elegance of movement, that's built around dance and freewheeling basketball? Or is there a natural dimension to it all? Who knows?

The writer Roy Blount Jr. looked around the Steelers locker room forty years ago and what he saw then is what's there today. The blacks are better muscled, tighter, quicker, more adept, and more adroit. He could have added that they move with more of what you'd have to call style and even wit. They play a fast, hard-hitting, elegant, and spirited game, high flying and gutsy.

The prowess of black players has changed football in much the way it changed basketball. The Celtics star Bill Russell recalls playing against an all-white team when he was in college. The white team was methodical and disciplined: Their coach wouldn't even allow them to leave the ground to shoot a jump shot. Russell's black-dominated team flew high and higher and won by about a hundred points—though Russell, being one of the more stubborn guys alive, couldn't help admiring the stubborn opposition coach, who stuck to his guns and prohibited that frivolous innovation, the outside jumper.

Watching pro football with my father in the early 1960s, there was plenty to admire. But the game could devolve into a spectacle of slow, overweight white men pushing each other around in mud. Pro football sometimes looked like a group shoving match outside a Somerville bar, or like a bunch of guys trying to force an invisible refrigerator one way while another bunch tried to shove it back at them. Jim Brown and a few others lit the scene up, sure, but before blacks got to football in significant numbers it was a slower, sloppier game. Some of the guys on the line weren't really athletes—they were simply big (though often they were mean enough). When pro and college football took in black players in significant numbers, the game changed: It got faster, more glamorous, more dangerous, and a lot more fun to watch.

The game changed slowly, though. Jim Brown says that when he entered the league in 1957, each team held itself to six or maybe eight black players. There had to be an even number, Brown says, so that the blacks could room together on the road. If there were seven, a white guy would have to room with a black and that wasn't acceptable. Brown remembers a time when the Cleveland Browns went on the road and left an injured black player at home. "Rather than pair off the extra black with the extra white, management bought each player a separate room. They were willing to pay for an additional room in order to preserve the color line." But matters have changed and now the National Football League is predominantly black.

It's not easy for an outsider to see inside the players' culture of the NFL, but it's possible that more and more it's becoming a black culture in which the white players need to be accepted by the blacks if they're going to thrive on the team. It seems that at least sometimes they need to be accepted *as black*. A white lineman was charged with harassing a black player, calling him, among other things a "half-nigger." The white lineman's black teammates jumped to back him up. "Richie's honorary," one defender said to a white questioner. "I don't expect you to understand because you're not black. But being a black guy, being a brother is more than just about skin color. It's about how you carry yourself. How you play. Where you come from. What you've experienced. A lot of things."

Standing in the University of Virginia locker room at halftime during a game against Duke, I heard a memorable exchange between a white offensive lineman (300 pounds) and a black one (340 or so). Virginia was ahead (for the time being) and both were in high spirits. "Hey," said the larger, "it was all good. But did you see that? I got knocked flat by a 220-pounder. Now that is humiliating." Said his colleague by way of consolation: "Hey, at least you're black." Surely being both white *and* knocked on your ass by a 220-pound slip of a guy would be more than any self-respecting O-lineman could bear.

What happened on Thanksgiving Day, the great Malden-Medford clash of 1969? They ran us over. They were too big and fast and they had so much talent that they played in two platoons, offense and defense. We'd never encountered this before. Johnny Joy played brilliantly—he picked off a pass and made his share of tackles. But the whole Malden team played brilliantly. We stayed in the game longer than the oddsmakers would have predicted (if oddsmakers took an interest in high school ball). At halftime they were only up by a touchdown. But then they brought in their star fullback, who'd been down with an injury and doubtful. (He'd been in a car accident—head to windshield.) They ran the ball time after time, and slowly they began to wear us down.

But we gave them a fight. Our defense held a long while. Our star quarterback swept right and swept left and got the snot banged out of him but gained yardage. He completed some passes too, and our junior running back, who hadn't played much, emerged in the game and showed what he could do.

Still, they were too much for us—they won by twenty points, 26-6. Was Johnny Joy their star? They seemed to have so many exceptional players that it was almost embarrassing, but Johnny was one who stood out.

How did we hang in against them so long? Who knows? But maybe our coach's riffs about Johnny had a little to do with it. He'd taken what was there for him to use and used it. We were a bunch of white guys who needed to get juiced up. So he made it a white-black game as well as he could. And Johnny gave him a little help by spray-painting his moniker in flashy swirls on the stadium wall. (If it was Johnny who did it. Who knows—it could have been anyone.) White against black! Us against them!

After the game the coaches came around to each of us seniors and thanked us for our efforts. The head coach couldn't think of much to thank me for other than not missing practice much. The assistant coach who had gotten mildly, then more than mildly obsessed with Johnny Joy muttered his line about our turkey tasting like a baloney sandwich. Rick Strong said that his turkey was going to taste fine.

For the Malden players it was different, naturally. The team had not only beaten us, their main rivals; they'd also copped the Greater Boston League championship, the championship that Medford had owned a couple of seasons before. They went roaring off the field with their coach perched on their shoulders. He clasped his hands and waved them over his head like a boxing champ—enjoying the triumphal ride far more than our coach had done the day we managed to beat Somerville. Out of the corner of my eye I believe I caught Johnny walking slowly off the field, head hung, shoulders dipped. He looked as though he'd lost the game. My buddies from Malden told me later that he was mad at the coach, mad at the team. He'd wanted to play more (maybe go both ways), get the ball more; he was planning to be a real football star—go on to college, maybe become a pro. Now the season was over and he hadn't been able to show what he could do. He felt the dream was evaporating in front of him.

That Thanksgiving Day I followed the example of many other seniors and took my game jersey, stained from a dunk in the mud (though not one caused by Johnny), and shoved it deep in my gym bag. It was a tradition for seniors to swipe their game jerseys, though some of us got frisked on the way out by the coaches and had to give them back. I made it out with mine, no problem.

If you were to take a visitor from a faraway land to catch a pro football game, what might he see? He'd be confused to begin with: Football can be as complicated as cricket, and explaining it to a novice takes developed pedagogical powers, and patience to boot. But if the traveler stopped listening to the patter about first downs and offsides, shotgun formation and the pistol, and simply looked, he might come to a distressing conclusion. Yes, I see what this is about. This is a spectacle that features strong, young black men beating the hell out of each other. Rich white men (and a few others) watch from the luxury booths and the stands as the players turn their bodies into weapons and send them against each other at bullet speed. The audience delights in the hits. They delight when the hit is a white man on another white man, sure. But the guys who take most of the big-time pops, the running backs and the wide receivers, and the players who deliver them, the d-backs and linebackers, are mostly black.

There's a scene in Ralph Ellison's novel *Invisible Man* that may, a bit hyperbolically, begin to illustrate what's happening on Saturday and Sunday afternoons in the fall. *Invisible Man* begins with a sequence that no one who encounters it forgets, the Battle Royal.

The white grandees of a certain Southern county gather regularly for a ritual. It's males-only in the spectator's ring—and it draws shady characters as well as some of the county's supposedly respectable. Our narrator is surprised to see the superintendent of schools, whom he took to be a man of exceptional probity. There's drinking and cigar smoking and ribald stories and, at the center of the gathering, a beautiful tall woman, naked, there to be ogled by all. But then comes the main event. Ten young boys, all black, stripped down to their shorts, wearing boxing gloves, get shoved into a ring. They have blindfolds on. They can't see each other or the assembled company. They can't feel anything either, at least until the signal sounds and they go to work in the Battle Royal, trying to beat the life out of each other.

They swing and smash and duck and run. They get clobbered in the stomach, banged in the head, pushed to the ground and kicked. The blindfolds make it quite a show. If the fighters flag or try to hide, the white men in the audience urge them on, sometimes with a kick or a punch. But mostly the black boys go at each other, not needing much encouragement. In time, the narrator's blindfold drops a quarter inch and he can half-see the melee. His mouth is full of blood; his guts ache from a wallop; but on he fights. What choice does he have? "Everyone fought hysterically. It was complete anarchy. Everybody fought everybody else."

The Battle Royal goes on an unbearably long time. When it does pause, matters get no better for the narrator. He's forced to fight the biggest and most aggressive of the boys, who beats what's left of him soundly. All the while our hero is wondering one thing: When will I get to deliver the edifying speech on the Negro and his future in America that I'm slated to give?

Finally the pummeling is over and it's time for the boys to get their reward. The white men roll out a mat covered with treasure. There are dollar coins, high-denomination bills, and gold pieces. There are gold pieces! The boys leap forward—even our narrator does. But as he touches a coin he reels back. The mat is wet; there's an electric charge crackling through. But the boys want that money anyway. They dive and they take the shocks. They squirm and shake with pain, but they gather what they can from the buzzing floor. The white men on the periphery roar with pleasure. This is almost as amusing as the Battle Royal. It's wonderful, absolutely wonderful, what kinds of entertainment these boys provide.

When the rewards have been distributed, our narrator gets to deliver his speech on Negro advancement. For his pains, he receives an envelope containing a letter awarding him a full scholarship to the local all-black college.

Ellison's Battle Royal scene isn't subtle. Nor is the scene a slice of conventional realism. It's dreamlike, allegorical. And its allegorical power can lead you into another view of what black men are doing on Saturday and Sunday afternoons on top-tier college and especially on pro football fields. (The writer Gregg Easterbrook also points to this scene in his illuminating book on football, *The King of Sports*.) Perhaps Ellison's scene is the bitter side of those feats of grace and daring that we celebrate. Every autumn Sunday provides America with a sequence of Battles Royal.

Well, maybe so, you might reply. But you can't say the guys out on the football field are being exploited, can you? Pro football players are rich. They live like royalty. They buy blazing cars, palace dwellings; they throw parties the way Darius of Persia did. No one glues their dollars to the carpet; no one puts counterfeit currency in their hands. They live like kings.

Or they do if they last. A five-year career in the pros is a triumph. A running back averages two and a half. Every week in college ball and the pros there are career-ending injuries. A kid works his whole life with the dream of playing big-time football. He digs in to make a tackle, his foot gets stuck in the turf, his knee twists and fails—dream gone. Or he simply finds, as Johnny Joy seemed to have done, that he's not as good as he thought, or that the coaches don't value him the way he thinks they should. The game draws players in and chews them up. What does NFL stand for? Ask the players; they know: Not For Long.

Some players emerge with princely wealth, sure. But will princely wealth give you back the knees you had as a boy, before other men stoked on steroids decided to knock them out from under you time after time? Will it return the grip to a hand that's been stepped on repeatedly, sometimes intentionally, sometimes not? Most of all, what can wealth do to repair a brain that has been concussed a half-dozen times? Said one former pro football player: I used to be afraid that my body would be so stiff and sore that I couldn't pick up my three-year-old son. Now I'm afraid that someday soon I won't be able to recognize him. What can we do about someone whose emotional life is now dominated by alternating bouts of depression and rage? "Canst thou not minister to a mind diseased?" asks Shakespeare's grieving king. Even now, with our advances in medical technology, we must answer: not too readily, not too well.

The star defensive end of the Miami Dolphins, Jason Taylor, talks about a year in the pros when he nearly had to have his leg amputated. He played game after game with a catheter running from his armpit to his heart. His calf oozed blood for so long that he had to have the equivalent of a drain installed. One day the pain was so bad that he lay down in the parking lot in front of his doctor's office, got into the fetal position, and cried like a child.

All of these things happen to the white men who play the game, sure. It's football. But as the pro and big-time college game has become more populated by African Americans, it's also become faster, more hard-hitting, and more dangerous. Players weigh much more than they used to—it's said that the year the Jets won the Super Bowl against the Colts there was only one three-hundred-pounder in the league, and he was embarrassed to admit it. Now, you probably can't play offensive line unless you weight three hundred plus, and more poundage is usually welcome. Steroids and human growth hormone, combined with sophisticated weight training, have made players way faster and stronger than they were when my dad and I camped in front of our console TV. They can deliver a lot more hurt than they could during the days of slow-motion mud-ball.

The pro game is dangerous for blacks and for whites too, sure—but the NFL is now 70 percent black. It's mostly blacks playing the modern professional game and sustaining the risks. At a certain point, the point at which money enters the equation and begins to dominate it, football changes. It becomes much less about character and courage and loyalty, though those qualities may still matter. The game becomes less about education and more about profit—and it also becomes brutally dangerous to body and to soul.

We know more and more now about the risks of football and many of us are distressed by them. But maybe the risks also *add* to our appreciation of the game. The men on the field risk destroying themselves out of pure spirit—love of fame, love of wealth, and love for the intensity of football. They are doing something amazing, these (mainly) black males. They're behaving like men. They are doing what manly individuals have traditionally done, fighting for their place in the world. They are showing physical prowess and physical bravery. They're risking everything to get to the top.

The rest of us often live our lives by degrees. We spend our days calculating, and then we recalculate our calculations. We are careful, circumspect. Is prudence what the poet said—an ugly old maid courted by incapacity? No matter, we are prudent. We sit at our computer terminals and live our lives secondhand. We watch our TVs, hum along to our personal playlists, and gaze enchanted at our action movies. But these men, these pro football players, actually live. They live with immediacy. They're fully present and (until someone knocks them sideways) they're one with themselves. They know exactly what they want to do: star and win, and they're willing to take risks to do it.

Perhaps we watchers sometimes feel that we barely live at all, and need others to live our lives as men for us. In gratitude we will turn over a percentage of our resources to them. We'll allow them, or some of them, to grow gaudily rich.

And the black men who surge to the game, are they victims in all this?

Everyone who steps up to play on the big-time college and professional level knows what the risks are: NFL/Not For Long (also: No Fun League). By the time a player reaches his fourth year of college he's often been down on his knees praying that his teammate will be all right, that his teammate will walk again. He knows this could happen to him.

But on the players come anyway—they're hungry to take the field. They line up for the Sunday Battle Royal. They sacrifice their bodies for the American viewing public. So some black rappers chant about taking their AK-47s out to the street and killing their enemies, other black men, whom they call niggers. *Bang* comes the sound of a shotgun blast. "These niggas is still fuckin' talking? You niggas still breathing? Fuckin' roaches!" Then the shotgun booms again. That's Tupac Shakur on one of the best-known rap CDs, *The Don Killuminati: The 7 Day Theory.* The image of blacks being brave, the image of blacks ruining each other, the image of black-on-black war: It sells. White people buy it and blacks do too.

For some time, black males have had the role of representing manliness in America. The writer Norman Mailer called his adventurous hipster, the 1950s existential hero who risked it all traversing the night side of the American dream, the White Negro. Mailer writes, "One is Hip or one is Square . . . one is a rebel or one conforms, one is a frontiersman in the Wild West of American nightlife, or else a Square cell, trapped in the totalitarian tissues of American society, doomed willy-nilly to conform if one is to succeed . . . So it is no accident that the source of Hip is the Negro for he has been living on the margin between totalitarianism and democracy for two centuries."

In the nineteenth century there was a phenomenon called blackface minstrelsy (memorably described by Eric Lott in a book called *Love & Theft*). In the minstrel shows, white performers smeared their faces black and went onstage to prance lewdly, thrust out their pelvises, and waggle their behinds. They assumed a freedom to be raunchy and raw that was foreclosed to purportedly civilized whites—a freedom to be (what they imagined as) black.

The White Negro is a white guy's concoction. The blackface minstrel show was usually white conceived, white directed, and white cast (though sometimes, black men would cork up their own faces and go on stage). Now pro football—probably our culture's main source for images of manliness—is frequently directed and starred in (coached and played) by African Americans themselves.

When you step into a black high school in inner-city Philly or Boston or New York and you ask the boys what they intend to do when they go out into the world, they don't have much doubt. They are going to be pro athletes; they are going to be professional entertainers. They're going to be hip-hop stars; they're heading for the NBA or the NFL. But of course that won't happen for most of them. (In the Malden yearbook, I see a picture of Johnny Joy helping to make a ferocious tackle on our quarterback, but I see nothing about his going on to college or even graduating from the high school.) Many young black men will be going to prison or otherwise be absorbed into what's called the criminal justice system. (There are a million and a quarter black men in jail; millions more are on probation or in halfway houses.) A few, though—a few—will be out there on Saturday, then out there on Sunday. A few—a few—will be on records rapping, sometimes about money and hos and about blowing away other black men, "niggas."

If education by football (or basketball or rap) is the only education that's available to you, or the only kind you can respond to, you may be in a bad way. How about Ralph Waldo Ellison and *Invisible Man*? the schoolteacher in me wants to ask; and then on to R. W. Emerson and Whitman and Frost and Dickinson and James Baldwin and Zora Neale Hurston and Donne and Shakespeare? (Did Johnny Joy ever get a chance to look at these books, or was it all football?) How about rising through the exertion of the mind and not the breaking of bodies? How about thinking to the point where you can see and analyze your situation and maybe do something about it?

Hide the scandal in plain sight if you want it to disappear—everyone knows that much. Pro football is at least in part about black people blasting each other at the stadium and on TV. Sure, there are white players. (Many of them are circumspect enough to be offensive linemen—they last the longest.) But it is mostly about blacks. The ones who take the big hits—the runners and receivers—are almost exclusively black. The knockout hitters—

the reckless defensive backs and the detonating linebackers—are usually black too. It is black Battle Royal, for which many black people cannot wait to sign up. And in what is supposedly post-racial America, it's a spectacle that white Americans savor.

A certain kind of college education by football is deceiving a lot of young black men and their families. Come, the recruiter says, play for us—play for Alabama, play for Michigan, play for the Ohio State University. You'll get a free education and a direct route to the NFL. It's yours for the taking. (Look at all the gold coins on the carpet.) Many of the kids are poor; they're dying for a break and their families need a lift too. But four years later, you're not going to the NFL (most won't be); you don't have any-thing like an education (you took an athlete's course schedule and it's likely you didn't graduate); you may walk with a limp and possess a memory that's no longer quite in working order. The head coach in college—your football educator, who is almost in-evitably white—makes more than a million dollars a year.

Yet what guys do on the field is beautiful—beautiful and dar-ing. Ballplayers live life rather than contemplating it. They get off their chairs and perform feats that are nothing less than amazing. The rest of us watch in admiration and envy and awe. When these men, these ballplayers come to the end of their lives, they will at least be able to say that for some period they actually *lived*.

I heard that at the end of Malden's championship season they held a banquet to celebrate and they gave Johnny Joy a game ball from the contest with Medford. But I heard that Johnny was still angry with the team for not granting him the recognition he deserved. He was mad at the coaches for making him a defensive back and not letting him run with the ball. After the banquet was over, the story went, Johnny stepped out into the middle of the street and chucked the ball as far as he could. He threw that football far, far away. It was a beautiful toss, I'll bet, long and spiraling sweetly into the dark. Then he walked away by himself, hurt and alone, with no one beside him.

8

TEARING UP THE TOWN: LOYALTY

One Saturday night after my senior season was over, a few of my fellow football players and I decided it might be fun to smash the plate glass windows at Brigham's Ice Cream parlor in Medford Square. We'd been drinking. We'd been drinking quite a lot— six beers, eight beers, maybe ten apiece. (It was always a point of pride to get into double figures.) We were bored and looking for something to do. The idea of smashing the windows was an unusual one for us. We generally didn't go in for vandalism, though a number of us, including me, didn't mind getting into street brawls, either one-on-one or all in, with as many as twenty guys swinging and smacking (and hitting the ground) at the same time.

The night we started talking about breaking the windows, we were perched up on a rocky promontory over the city, looking down on Medford Square and the lights below, which were winking out. It was late Saturday night, soon to be Sunday morning, winter and unusually warm. The football season was over, and the four of us were missing the game. We were bored. We needed something exciting to do—something as exciting as running back a kick or sacking a quarterback in front of a few thousand people. Maybe we were mourning the loss of the game and the team and looking for something that would create the kinds of feelings in us that football had. We'd been part of a band, a tribe, a pack, and now that was fading. We were going to do what we could that night to restore the old feeling, though in a dark and pretty dangerous way. And I was going to learn something about loyalty and the game of football.

It wasn't unusual for me to be out sitting around and drinking with fellow football players on a weekend night. I had other friends, for sure. But partway through my junior season, when I was finally confirmed as one of the players—a kid who "likes to hit"—I began spending more and more of my free time with guys from the team. I had plenty of free time that year. I hated school. I usually did no homework, or as little as possible. I was almost always available to go out and cruise around in someone's car, drinking as much beer as I could hold and looking for diversion.

One night during my junior year five of us ballplayers loaded ourselves into a GTO owned by a guy we called Sap, Fran Sapienza. Sap loved to drive around the square in his GTO, cruising past Brigham's with the Beach Boys, the Temptations, or the Beatles turned up loud. We sat in Sap's GOAT, as it was called, with beers between our legs, peering out the window for cops.

When the coast seemed clear, we lifted and chugged at high speed, then jerked our cans down, often with a splash. (After doing this a few times, we would be wet in exactly the wrong place.) We hollered out the window, issuing invitations to girls we did not know and hearty greetings to girls that we did. We threw our hands out the window when we recognized friends, whom we wanted to recognize us cruising in a high-prestige vehicle.

One night Frank Richie, 250-odd pounds and sitting on my lap in the backseat, made an announcement. "Medford sucks!" he said. "Let's get out of here." Get out of here! To where? Almost no one we knew was inclined to leave Medford, especially spontaneously on a Saturday night. Brigham's parking lot was the center of the solar system; we revolved round it like obedient planets. Then too, Medford may have sucked—it was gritty, small, boring, and all the rest—but no one ever came out and said as much.

Richie was his own guy. He was a defensive tackle and at the beginning of my junior year, everyone figured he was the next big thing. He was strong and mean, and he had the presence of a brown bear recently out of hibernation, looking for food, ready to fight. When you spoke to him, it was as though you'd just woken him up from satisfying sleep. He was at least mildly pissed at you for it, almost no matter what you said. Richie had come back for what was to be his star senior year thirty pounds over-weight and he did nothing to remedy the situation. He ran his sprints in slow motion. He refused to really employ the ridiculous isometric machine, the Exer-Genie, we were supposed to use before practice. It was a thick metal cylinder and you pulled a rope attached to a crossbar through it, first in a squat, then in a curl, then in an overhead press. Richie delighted in grunting and groaning and finally screaming his way through an Exer-Genie set; then, when the next guy picked up the rope, he discovered that Richie had put about five pounds of resistance on the machine. When the coaches spoke to Richie, he responded as though they were bill collectors.

The night we left Medford, we were reasonably merry—not like the night we smashed the Brigham's windows. There was something evil in the air that night. The night we left Medford was a regular football-guys night. The only difference was that Richie had a strong idea, and when Richie had a strong idea, you either went along or got into a fight with him.

Richie gave instructions, and Sap being Sap, he complied. We went to the package store, where Richie bought two cases of beer without showing an ID. We stowed most of the beer in the trunk of the GOAT and then got back in and repositioned ourselves, Richie again on my lap. I told Richie that it might have made more sense for me to be the top guy in the configuration, weighing as I did sixty pounds less. Richie answered that such an arrangement would make him less comfortable.

Richie announced that we were going to drive to Cape Cod. He informed Sap that to his knowledge the record run from Malden, where we'd scored the beer, to the Cape was one hour and three minutes. Sap was happy to accept the challenge.

And about an hour and one minute later, we made it over the Bourne Bridge. We had passed every car we could have passed and a couple that I was sure we could not. We drove often in our own lane. But for extended periods we drove in the oncoming lane because it was empty and there was more room. Sap drove so fast that even Richie, who was given to griping and raging on sundry subjects most of the time, shut his mouth. At one point he clung to my knees in what I can only imagine was fear.

When we got to the Cape we got a room in a motel. We brought the beer in and we drank it. All of it. We talked about football: football practice, the coaches, the games we'd won that year, and the games we'd lost. By five in the morning the beer was gone. We chucked the empties out the window into the yard behind the motel, got back into the GOAT, and returned to Medford at a speed that was not record breaking but was still brisk enough. Richie sat on my lap.

The Cape night was a road trip version of what we football players did all the time. We got together in bunches and cruised around drinking beer, or if no car was available, we sat outdoors at a park—sometimes in arctic temperatures—drinking and talking. By my senior year some of us had added weed to the mix, but most of the Medford football players had made commitments to Schlitz or to Budweiser. Much was made of staying true to your brand; much was made, less directly, of staying true to the team.

From time to time we got into fights, sometimes (though rarely) with each other; sometimes with kids from other schools;

on one occasion with a bunch of kids from Charlestown, who gave us more than we could handle. But mostly we sat and talked and, if we were outside, swung on the park swings, or climbed to the top of the jungle gym and dared each other to jump off—it was high.

At the end of my junior year we talked about the season that had ended (not so well, at five and four) and the season that was about to start. We talked about the coaches. We tarred the head coach with insults—he was a cold, Tom Landry type, all about the Xs and Os. We gossiped about the younger coaches, the position coaches, all of whom had played college ball—the highest achievement known to us. We talked about who the strongest of the linemen was; who had the most balls and the least; who should have played more and who should have had a permanent seat on the bench. Then we drank some more and continued talking.

We should have been out with our girlfriends, probably. But few of the ballplayers had girlfriends. We preferred the company of the other males. We preferred the company of the pack. This wouldn't surprise certain social scientists at all. It surely wouldn't surprise Lionel Tiger, whose name should have gone to an ace defensive back, but which ended up instead attached to a perceptive anthropologist from Rutgers. It was Lionel Tiger who made the term "male bonding" a cultural meme in the late sixties. If Lionel Tiger had seen us drinking and talking by and on the jungle gym, he would have been pleased. He would certainly have reminded us that jungle gyms are also called monkey bars.

Yes, Tiger would no doubt say, we were probably participating in something like primate behavior. Back before cities and churches and kings on golden thrones, human beings roamed the plains of the world, seeking sustenance. The males hunted; the females gathered and waited for the men to return with the meat. And to secure that meat the males had to learn to act together: No single hunter, no matter how adept, could take down a wooly mammoth alone. Hunting in the early phases of human life was—well, it was a team sport. So men had to learn how to function in groups. They needed leaders, some kind of hierarchical order, and they needed to figure out how to coordinate their efforts to kill the mammoth or fend off the saber-tooth. There was a great deal at stake—male cooperation brought in the food. But it also seems, at least to some archaeologists, that for a while it was an open question whether the human species would defeat the tigers and the mastodons, or whether these fierce creatures would win out and rid the world of humans. Every steak dinner we eat now is a tacit celebration of the human victory over the ancient predators. We won. They lost.

Men needed to learn how to bond in order to survive, and over time this capacity became nearly instinctive, or so Professor Tiger suggests. Getting together and forming a functioning group with leaders and followers and even a semi-outcast on hand to illustrate what sort of behavior won't be tolerated was critical to the development of the human species. (In Homer's *Iliad* an ugly, misshapen soldier named Thersites plays the role of the outcast, displaying the inverse of the heroic qualities warriors like Achilles and Hector embody.) Group bonding continues to matter. When human beings go to war, or begin a major business venture, or come together to try to cure cancer or defeat Alzheimer's, they've got to be able to go into group mode. Those cultures in which people can effectively merge into groups will survive and thrive; those that cannot will decline. The writer Luigi Barzini claims that his own people, the Italians, whom he clearly loves, have simply never been able to achieve full group cohesion—thus the relative failures that have come to pass when they've tried to conduct modern warfare or create a high-functioning postindustrial state.

What were we doing cruising around in Sap's GOAT? What were we doing swinging on the monkey bars, one hand gripping the highest rung, a bottle of Bud (or Schlitz) in the other? We'd say we were fucking around, of course. We'd probably say that we were wasting time. But Lionel Tiger might tell us that we were doing the rather lazy, relatively passive part of male bonding. We were getting ready to play football together. And we were also getting ready to function later in life, when we had to form a team and get something done that none of us could manage alone. We were educating ourselves for football and letting football educate us for the future.

There's no way that Richie could have let me take the dominant position in the back of the GOAT. He was a senior; I, a junior. Hierarchy had to be observed and enforced. Teams need senior leadership. If the next year I were in a similar position with a junior ballplayer, I would have to perch on his lap as

Richie did on mine. It didn't really matter whether Richie was mean and took pleasure in my pain. (I think he did.) He was doing his male-bonding, hierarchy-creating job. If I'd challenged him on it, he would have fought me, and from Lionel Tiger's point of view, it would have been the right thing to do.

Not for nothing do so many Wall Street firms and high-powered law offices want to hire guys (and now women) who have played team sports—even if they aren't the smartest characters to submit a résumé. These people can get together and form a group and the group can make something happen. They understand, almost intuitively, the dynamics of collective effort.

The problem is that what happens when people, especially males, get into groups is often undesirable. The same complex bonding that brings down a charging behemoth with no loss of human life has other applications. Men in groups who have established the necessary bonds are dangerous, and so, at times, were we.

I still can't say for sure whose idea it was to smash the Brigham's windows. There were four of us that night; it could have come from anyone. One of the players was a star—a terrific receiver, a speedster, who ran with a jaguar stride. (This stride would be his undoing.) The two other ballplayers were linemen like me, guys who loved a can of beer and then another and another. (Like me.)

Sitting up on that promontory over the Brigham's parking lot, looking down at the city as the lights winked out and Saturday night slid into Sunday morning, we began to talk about how much we hated this and hated that. We hated math; we hated English; we hated various coaches of ours who had stood between us and our chances for more glory. But it turned out that what we hated most at that moment was the apparently innocuous ice cream parlor at our feet. Why did we hate it? Brigham's was the vortex of social life at our high school. It was where the pretty girls and the popular guys were to be found after school and on Friday nights. It was where some guys challenged each other to fight and where other guys got "shot down" by the girls they'd been mooning over. Brigham's was where you learned where you stood in the high school hierarchy. What you generally discovered at Brigham's was that if you took your own assessment and divided by two, you pretty much had it.

Someone issued a dare. Someone demurred. (It was me, honest.) There was talk about who had balls and who didn't and who could acquire evidence of them right now. At a certain point in the conversation, our legs still dangling innocently down the rock ledge like the legs of ten-year-old boys dangling over a swimming hole in summer, the idea took hold. And five minutes later, it was no longer an idea; it was a plan of action. Male bonding was complete; the group dynamic was in play—or so Professor Tiger might have told us. It was time to break some windows.

My three comrades went along the promontory searching for suitably sized chunks of rock. It wasn't hard to find them: This was stony New England, where the glacier had come down and cracked the earth's crust into jagged chunks. My friend the receiver raised his up over his head as though it were a ten-pound football and he'd crossed the end zone with it in his hands. He did an elegant victory jig. And it was probably about then that I realized that this window business was really going to happen. Maybe it was the sight of my buddy dancing like a Cro-Magnon ready for combat with the tribe one valley away. Or maybe it was because my alcohol fuzz was fading and being replaced, slowly, slowly, by access to what the teachers and the counselors and the priests think of as the reality principle.

"Fuck this!" I bellowed, or something like it. "This is really stupid."

My friends did not listen to me. I'm not sure that they even heard. They were busy picking out rocks of the right heft and the right weight. My friends were ready to go. They were alight with the furor that we reached before a game, when we stood on the field doing our calisthenics and had worked ourselves up into a collective rage. Beat Somerville! we screamed. Beat Somerville! But by the end of the drill all pretense was gone. Kill! Kill! Kill Somerville! we chanted. But now we had no more games to play and no more Alabama Quick Cals to execute.

I hollered and entreated and cried out to them and at last one seemed to hear what I was saying. "You don't have to do shit," Joe, one of my fellow linemen, replied. "There are only three windows!"

He was right. There were only three windows—actually two windows and a glass door. And when Joe said this, I felt a strange exhilaration. Because on some level I did want those windows broken. I did want the plan to move to fruition. I wanted to be part of the exploit. Maybe this is only human: When we see an action about to unfold, no matter how dire its consequences are likely to be, there's a part of us that needs to see it consummated. We want to discover what will happen and then what will happen later because of it. "I love disaster," as the rock song goes, "and I love what comes after."

I sat on the top of the promontory and took in the spectacle. I watched as the split end loped down the street with his jaguar stride and gently lofted a stone through the first window. (I wasn't alone, it turned out. Someone else saw the rock go through that window. Someone else saw that perfect football stride, but couldn't quite place it—couldn't exactly remember where he'd seen it before.) I heard the smash of the door as my second buddy hit it, and I saw glass froth out like champagne bubbles. (The door was on a curve and I couldn't actually see the rock strike.) Then came the final smash, which echoed up and down empty High Street like an artillery blast—for this was the grandest of the windows, the one that you peeked into to see who was there and who was not and how crowded the booths were and who was on at the soda fountain. I heard the ordnance smash, and then I heard the store alarm go off. It swirled up and down the street and around and back like a boomerang.

———

Most people who have written influentially about groups don't much care for them. Lionel Tiger stands out for having something like a double perspective on what happens when men get together and bond. Often, he suggests, groups produce admirable results—hunting, successful warfare, research, and many forms of civilized collaboration. But he knows the dark side of male groups too. At certain points a bunch of men together can stop being a group and become a pack. They can rape and kill and destroy for no apparent reason. They wreak havoc. Tiger seems not really sure why this happens—why the chemistry of the male bond goes out of kilter—but like everyone, he is well aware that it does.

Other prominent writers who have thought about groups have had a hard time seeing their positive side. Friedrich Nietzsche in particular despised what he called the herd mentality. It was a direct result, he felt, of many of the other developments that took place in nineteenth-century Europe that he also detested. The herd mentality went along with democracy, socialism, feminism, the rise of newspapers, and the decline of serious education. In one of his books, Nietzsche has a particularly nasty portrait of the kind of man who clings to the herd mentality. He calls him the Last Man. The Last Man is small and timid and he goes hopping and blinking through life. He's afraid to lead; he's afraid to hatch a new idea. He lives to get his meager sustenance and after he's finished for the day, he administers a dose of narcotic to himself. Nietzsche was probably thinking about alcohol, which he despised. But TV, video games, and movies would no doubt qualify for him too. The Last Man has his "little poison for the day and [his] little poison for the night." He avoids quarrels, which tend to spoil digestion. The Last Man lives longest, says Nietzsche, in part because he'll never risk his life for a high cause. "His race," says Nietzsche, "is as ineradicable as the flea beetle." The Last Man loves the safety of the group. He loves the world in which there is "no shepherd and one herd."

Freud followed after Nietzsche, denouncing the herd mentality in a potent book called *Group Psychology and the Analysis of the Ego*. But unlike Nietzsche's assessment, Freud's analysis of group behavior focuses on the leader. For Freud, getting into a group and coming under the sway of the leader is much like being hypnotized. He believed that the group leader usurps the highest mental function of the group members—he takes the place of their reason and conscience. He tells the group what's good and bad, true and false, right and wrong. Most of the time, the group mind is regressive. At political rallies people act like children under the direction of a commanding figure, the sort of person we're inclined to call an alpha male. (If there was an alpha male in our rock-tossing group, it was no doubt the wide receiver.) That figure can extract productive efforts from the group—it isn't impossible. But most of the time the group leader gets people acting in barbaric ways: He primes them for war; he feeds them on hate until they're ready to launch a pogrom or collaborate on a Final Solution.

Nietzsche and Freud thought that almost all consequential human achievement comes from individuals who work in isolation. Such people tend not only to be loners, but to be out of step with their contemporaries. Nietzsche wanted his work to create the mind of the future. He said that he wanted to be "untimely." The idea that groups could be good for much of anything was anathema to Freud and Nietzsche—and the two thinkers remain, after many years, critical to Western reflections about the group mind.

Freud lived to see many of his thoughts on group behavior borne out. *Group Psychology* came out in 1922. That was ten years before Hitler took power in Germany. Not long after the book's publication, a significant portion of the world went over to fascism and the cult of the leader: Hitler, Stalin, Franco, Tōjō, Mussolini. Freud's dark intimations about how humans behave in groups came true not only in Germany but also in Russia, Spain, Japan, and Italy. All over the world people got drunk on the idea of the leader. They gave over their superego—their unconscious sense of right and wrong—to posturing, yammering men, some of whom were probably half-insane. In not too long, fifty million people were dead.

Groups, small and large, are dangerous, especially when they are made up of men. Maybe Freud and Nietzsche can tell you why this is so and maybe they cannot. But that it *is* so, anyone can see.

———

Sunday morning, Joe and I skipped church and went cruising in his Plymouth Gold Duster down through Medford Square. We expected to see windows boarded up with plywood. We expected a crowd milling around Brigham's wondering who and why and what the fuck.

There was none of that. There were no crowds and no cops—it was Sunday at about eleven in the morning and there was almost no one on the street, most of Medford having gone off to church, or at least skipped it more discreetly than we had. The moms were cleaning the house of the weekend's mess; the dads were glomming around in their bathrobes, fighting their hangovers, getting ready for the Bruins or the Celtics to come on TV. And the windows were unbroken. Where there had been cannonball-sized holes in glass, there was gleaming surface. Had it been a dream? Had we gotten loaded and then popped a few more beers, made some plans about smashing windows, but been too stumbling drunk to do anything?

Joe and I pulled over in front of the ice cream shop, emerged from the car, and began studying the glass. Culprits are supposed to return to the scene of the crime, but I'm not sure many culprits have ever done it quite so quickly or exposed themselves as stupidly as we did. We tapped the glass a few times as though maybe it had been glued back together bit by bit and with a touch might fall back into crystals. Nope—seemed intact. But a bit too shiny. A bit too new. And probably—we told each other—it was new.

There had been no dream. Brigham's had simply gotten its act together fast, called the emergency glassworks, and had everything taken care of before the eleven-thirty mass began. It made sense. Vandalism begets vandalism and if certain Medford denizens had seen the blasted storefront they might have decided to do something similar down at the Pewter Pot Muffin House or Papa Gino's pizzeria. Or they might have elected to make window breaking a nightly diversion at Brigham's.

My pal and I went home, answered parental questions about the content of the eleven-thirty celebration of the Eucharist at Saint Raphael Parish, and brooded on what was going to happen next. But day followed day and by Friday of that week nothing had. There were rumors out there—or some. More and more people began to understand that four jocks had smashed the Brigham's windows. Kids were walking by me in the school corridor and making blasting sounds: *Kaboom! Kaboom! Kaboom!*

Late Friday afternoon, my phone rang. It was Joe, my lineman buddy, and he had an idea.

"Listen," he said, "there are a lot of rumors out there about the windows."

I agreed that there were.

"So, OK," Joe told me. "What we're going to do is this. We're going to go to the police station and we're going to let the cops know that we didn't do it."

"Are you kidding me?"

"No, no. They'll never think that if we did do it, we'd have the balls to walk into the station and deny it."

I told Joe that this was not a wholly sane way of thinking.

"The best part," he said, "is that you'll come too. There will be four of us and there were only three windows."

"And you think that'll throw the cops off."

"I know it will," Joe said. "There's no doubt about it."

Naturally I told Joe that this was a bizarre idea and that I wanted nothing to do with it. I told him that it wouldn't work and that the cops might lock us all up on the spot.

I hung up. I wanted no part of this idiotic plan. But I also felt terrible. I was going to let my buddies down. I was going to betray the team. I didn't know anything about Lionel Tiger, much less Sigmund Freud or Friedrich Nietzsche. I didn't understand the kind of force that group loyalty exerts on an individual. I didn't understand it, but I surely felt it.

In a few hours I was in the station house. Two of the cops we talked to were in their undershirts, just coming off the day shift. They were tired and cranky, but not unamused. Four high school guys had come to tell them they had not committed a crime. And one of those guys certainly had not. Given the way we carried ourselves, they might have been able to tell that the semi-innocent guy was me. They listened to us with bemusement but also with what seemed a weird admiration. They too knew something about hanging together. They knew something about loyalty, even of the rogue variety.

We told the cops that we had been in the proximity of Brigham's that night and we thought that we might have been seen and (wrongly, of course) identified as the culprits. One of the cops in an undershirt asked if we had been drinking. Joe admitted it. "Two beers," he said. "Two beers?" a cop in uniform asked. I noticed that he was doing something with his gun. "Two at the most," the wide receiver told him.

As the interview continued more cops drifted in. "Hey," one said to a newcomer, "these here guys? These guys here? These are the guys who *didn't* bust the windows over at Brigham's."

"So what are they doing here?"

"Excellent question."

We were lucky that the cops' shift had recently ended and they wanted to go home and that the night squad was (probably) off somewhere getting its briefing. If we'd arrived a little earlier or later we would have been a prime source of entertainment. It could have gone on quite a while and in a way you could readily imagine.

"Is there anything else you guys didn't do, just so's we know?"

"Yeah, that murder last year, down the Middlesex Fells, I'm guessing that wasn't you?"

"How about Kennedy? Hey, hey, make sure they didn't have anything to do with Kennedy down in Dallas neither."

They took it pretty easy on us. After only about fifteen minutes, we filed out of the police station, convinced that we had acquitted ourselves pretty darn well. Then we hopped into the Gold Duster and headed for the packy. We got a case of Schlitz and a couple of pints of hard liquor and repaired to one of the local parks to congratulate ourselves on our winning encounter with the Medford police force.

Eventually the guy who had seen the wide receiver loping down High Street placed the jaguar stride. He'd seen him catching passes over at Hormel Stadium, yes he had. He knew exactly who that strong runner was. The witness was an MDC policeman, a Metropolitan District Commission cop, one of the guys who had jurisdiction over state parks and highways. (MDC—we called them More Dumb Cops, but this guy clearly was not so dumb.) He let his brother officers at the Medford station house know who had been running on the street that night, and the game was over. Fathers were called on the phone; checks were written. Each window was a different price, with the largest one demanding a hefty check. The door was a bargain. Brigham's declined to press charges and the incident was over. We went back to drinking beer and fighting and talking and suspending ourselves one-armed and two- from the monkey bars.

Not all that much later a bunch of Medford cops would be prosecuted for committing one of the biggest bank jobs in American history. They did it a few blocks from the station, where we stood, denying a crime we hadn't been accused of committing. The cops spent an entire Memorial Day weekend inside the vaults of the Depositors Trust bank. They didn't find the cash they hoped for, so they began smashing the safety deposit boxes, which were full of money and jewelry. (Some of what they found, I was later told, belonged to people that it was not a good idea to steal from.) In all, they got loot worth twenty-five million bucks. I like to imagine that a few of the guys in the station room that night might have been involved. Did the crooked cops stand up for each other? Not in the long run, though for a while they tried.

What the hell were we doing there in that police station denying we'd done something that we hadn't been accused of doing? It was a ritual of a certain sort, I suppose. It was a loyalty ritual. We were performing a bonding rite. We were showing ourselves and whatever segment of the world cared to see that we Medford Mustangs stuck together. We fucked up together and then we defended ourselves as a bunch. No one squealed on anybody else. No one tried to shift blame. Our football education had involved lessons in loyalty and we had learned them.

It was important that all this took place after our playing time was done. Maybe football was over, but we were going to continue being loyal to each other down through time. We were Mustangs forever.

The night that the final discussion with the police took place—the night the checks were written—I wasn't on hand. When the cops asked once more if I'd been involved, my buddies said, as one: No, he didn't throw a rock. The cops didn't need to ask what I'd been doing at the station house. "He's a good friend," the police sergeant said to them. "He's a fucking idiot, though." Everyone laughed. In Medford "fucking idiot" could sometimes pass as a compliment.

Plants grow organically, serenely, and often beautifully. But human beings, even when they're making genuine progress in life, are often studies in uneven development. We're like cities where brilliant new apartments and universities are being constructed next to dilapidated, half-haunted houses. I still had enough anger and confusion in me to want to be part of that window-shattering spree. But other things were happening in my life too. I was becoming a reader, skipping school sometimes to hit the public library and push my nose into Hemingway and Faulkner. My grades were better—especially in English and history and my beloved philosophy course. I was beginning to see that some of the books I was reading seemed to be written for me personally. I didn't always understand Fitzgerald and Joyce and Faulkner and the rest, but I sensed that they might understand me pretty well, and in time I saw that was true.

I applied to college too, and I actually got admitted: first to Boston College (too expensive) and then off the wait list to the state university in Amherst. A well-connected neighbor helped with that one. When someone in my neighborhood acquired a TV or a washing machine from dubious sources, he'd say it had fallen off the back of a truck. That's where my acceptance to U Mass came from: It fell off the back of a truck. But I daresay I used it well enough.

My family pulled itself together too—at least some. My father never took ascetic vows, but he dialed some of his wild behavior back. (Or his body dialed it back for him—resilient as he was, there were only so many no-sleep, ten-beer nights he could handle.) My mother was never again the gentle, kindly soul she had been before my sister's death, but she became someone who could take some pleasure in life. When I was a boy my mother sang all the time, sweet Irish songs she'd learned from her mother. After Barbara's death, I never heard those songs again. My brother became an ace high school debater, got himself admitted to Amherst College, one of the best schools in the country, and has had a splendidly successful career in business and politics.

As for me, I suppose my main contribution to my family's survival was pulling myself together and not screwing up in any major ways. (Hey, I didn't actually chuck one of those rocks through the windows of Brigham's, did I?) My parents probably couldn't have taken it if I'd spiraled down and down, as I threatened to do. I saved myself—or rather philosophy and football saved me. I didn't really prop anyone else up—but I didn't need to. I just had to stay standing myself. I got over my grief for my sister's death and my guilt about it and I went on to make something of a life for myself. And as I did, I constantly thought back with pleasure to the camaraderie that I developed with a bunch of working-class guys on a five-and-four team in an unimportant city in the year of changes, 1969.

Surely those European sages had it right: Put them in groups and people, men especially, can act like beasts. Put them on football teams and they sometimes will. What we did was small potatoes compared to what football players frequently do. They get into fights and put other people in the hospital; they assault women; they commit gang rapes; they kill other guys or they come close. Football creates packs. Football creates men who are loyal to their tribe and despise everyone who is not a member. If you are not one of us, you do not really exist and (maybe) I can do to you what I want.

But there's something else too. I heard a story once, and I couldn't push it away, in part because one hears such stories all the time—and because it rang true, as true as the rape stories, as true as the assault stories that one also hears so often. One year a certain college football team was particularly close. The team's guys were always tight, but this was something special. The guys loved each other and it was clear that even after they graduated and after they went their ways, they'd always be a gang of brothers. One of them had a wife with serious mental problems; it went on for a long time and it was tough on everyone in the family. Three children, a husband from the team, and hard, hard times—but the husband had friends to rely on. And he did. His buddies talked to him on the phone. They came to visit. They guided him through as his wife got institutionalized one time, then another. For the man dearly loved his wife.

One bad morning she killed herself. By that evening there were seven former players sitting in the husband's living room with him. More were on the way. They dropped what they were doing and they came from every part of America to be with their friend, this bunch of guys with their herd mentality, with their group mind.

When my mother died three years ago, I had plenty of expressions of sympathy from the people around me, people I've worked with and lived by for thirty years. But the friends who helped the most, who spoke with the most feeling and the most warmth, often came from my past. Some of them were fellow ballplayers. No one listened better. No one spoke to me more directly about what it was to lose the most important person of my young life. No one wrote more movingly, though writing was not their medium. No one said things that mattered more, though I had not seen some of them face-to-face for twenty years. They helped me through, these tough and brutal guys; these guys with their herd mentality; guys locked down in their group mind.

CONCLUSION

FATHERS AND SONS

I grew up watching football with my father. Together we watched games in our tiny apartment in Malden and through football my father explained the world to me. A few people could be like Jim Brown, an athletic god. But many more of us could be like Y. A. Tittle. We could take what abilities we'd been given even if they were modest and work on them and work and work. We could do that in football, but we could do it in other pursuits too. We were all raw material, my father's message went, and though the material wasn't infinitely malleable, we could surprise ourselves by what would happen if we pushed on, shaping and reshaping.

I took in a lot from my father there in front of the TV set. (I suppose for us the television was the equivalent of the hearth or campfire where prior generations of fathers sat instructing sons in the arts of life.) So it should have been no surprise when, badly equipped as I was, I brought myself onto the field and tried to play. I achieved what I could, learned what I believed I might, and then, I thought, I left football and moved on to other matters. I thought that my football education was over.

The senior year philosophy class I took with Franklin Lears was like nothing I'd experienced. We read books that astonished me. We took up what seemed to be every worthwhile question under the sun. What is a good life? What is love—familial love, erotic love, love of country? What is justice? What is truth? And of course the one that perplexed me most then: Is it really better to receive harm than to do it? I thought that when I moved into the realm of books and ideas, I was moving away from football forever. This wonderful new territory that Frank Lears opened up was cerebral and refined in ways that my life on the football field never could be.

For a long time I thought that I had shed one skin for another. Once a jock, I became a thinker (or tried to be) and then (if only in aspiration) a writer. I believed that I left the game behind. But now, looking back, I'm not so sure. More and more I believe that football helped establish the basic elements of my identity, and that when I went off into my other life I took my football self with me. It was a fundamental part of what I was about. So it is, I suspect, for anyone who has played the game seriously. And I was serious—inept, but serious. I sometimes think that for me (and maybe a lot of other men too) football was what the economists call the base. All the rest was superstructure.

Like a lot of men I came to times in my life when I had to call on the kind of strength football helped me develop. I needed the resources that the game helped me to create. James Dickey has a marvelous poem about a dramatic moment when he had to draw on his former football strength. It's called "The Bee" and it's dedicated to the football coaches at Clemson University, where Dickey played ball. The poem is about football, but it's also about fathers and sons. I've probably read it thirty times.

It tells the story of how Dickey's son, who seems to be about six years old at the time, gets stung by a bee on the side of a California freeway. Overwhelmed with pain and fear, the boy goes running wildly into the traffic. It's up to his father to save him. Dickey is getting old; he's out of shape; he's not the guy he once was. But he flies into the freeway after his boy, and as he does he thinks of his old football coaches. "Backfield coach Shag Norton," he says, "tell me as you never yet have told me to get the lead out." In those fast-moving seconds, Dickey remembers his "spindling explosions through the five-hole"—he tries to bring back the resolve and strength he once commanded. And the old coaches help him: They "live in the air," he says; they "live in the ear." Then comes the most important line, at least to me: "They want you better than you are."

To save his son, Dickey has got to make the move that coaches warn you against as anything but a last resort. "I will have to leave my feet," he says. He does, and he grabs his son. "I have him where he lives." Old coaches rise up, Dickey says, when something must be saved. Their message is simple: Drive, dig, go for it. Try with all your might and then add more. They want you better than you are.

At the roadside after it's over, there's a sweet scene between

Dickey and his boy. It's time to step off the field and savor what we have. Time to look down on what Dickey calls "the man creating bruises of my arms." Time to take a breath.

As another poet says, "Strength attends us if but once we have been strong." Dickey, by his own account, was strong during those football days at Clemson, or at least he tried to be. (He seems to have had only a little more talent for the game than I did.) And if you've done it once, you can do it again. Old coaches live in the air.

It wouldn't surprise me to learn that Dickey called on the old coaches more than once. He eventually became famous, winning prizes for his poetry and writing the best-selling novel *Deliverance*. (He has a part in the film version, something he insisted on. He plays the sly Southern sheriff.) But for a long time Dickey's career didn't run smoothly. He was trapped in an advertising agency, Burke Dowling Adams, writing copy for Delta Air Lines, which he hated doing. One day he got news that he'd won a Guggenheim Fellowship. Not much later he walked out of the office, went home and shot his bow and arrow for a while, and then got down to writing poetry. The grant would last him only a year, and he had a family to sustain. But he struck ahead anyway and started a new life. I like to think that the old coaches were whispering in Dickey's ear when he walked out of his office that day too, urging him to take a chance, wanting him better than he was.

Nearly every man who has played ball and grown from it has, I'm sure, drawn on his former football-playing strength at one time or another. You get fired, you get divorced. Your child gets sick and you have to stop your life as it is and begin living for the child. And when it happens (and it happens to almost everyone) you have no idea where you'll find the strength you need. You go home and you look into your hands and you call on God or Jesus or your patron saint. And maybe that helps. But in my experience nothing helps you to fight a battle like having fought one before and come out OK. Bad luck befalls you and you never know how you're going to deal with it, because it seems like nothing comparable has occurred before. But then you think back and you hear the old coaches and you remember what you achieved on a ball field that maybe by rights you shouldn't have been on. Earlier you didn't know where you were going to get the strength but now—now maybe you do. "Diversity of strength attends us if but once we have been strong."

Tim Green, the former star defensive lineman for the Atlanta Falcons, has some worthwhile thoughts about the way football builds resilience. Football, he says, "teaches one thing that kids can't get anywhere else. It teaches them how to get knocked down and get back up. . . . We all know that all our lives we're getting knocked down. It happens to the richest, smartest and most famous people. The difference with a kid that plays football is that for the rest of his life he knows how to get back up. He knows from repetition that, hey, things happen, you get laid out. Football teaches kids to get up, over and over again, and that's why you see so many people in successful positions in life, not who played in the NFL, but who played football at some level as a kid and learned that lesson that stayed with them in everything else they did."

I'd give the last joint of a finger to have written "The Bee." But I know that his remarkable poems aren't Dickey's whole story. He was known as a drinker; he could be a braggart; he was a difficult father, though if you were going to go running into traffic full tilt, he was probably the father you wanted (assuming of course that "The Bee" is based on an actual event); he was an intimidating physical presence; for a while he chased anyone wearing a skirt in an effort to undo the situation as quickly as he could. By the time I met Dickey, in 1985 or so, he was a bloated ego, with his best work behind him—something he was way too smart not to know.

Who can really know another man? Who can see what's happening in his soul? But I wouldn't be surprised if those old coaches had a hand in inspiring not only Dickey's glory but also his decline. The good qualities that football helps implant can turn on you, and quickly. The man had guts—but how quickly guts can change into vainglory, aggression, and bullying.

I've called on the spirit of football in my life—of course I have. Though I've never had to summon it to deal with a crisis like the one Dickey describes in "The Bee." I've had some hard professional setbacks and I've seen people close to me get very sick. My response to these events wasn't perfect. But I did all right. The best of what I did was guided by many factors—I've been lucky and I've had a fine education—but football helped.

Past strength may attend you, even if you stumbled around acquiring it as much as I did.

But the temptation to smash through whatever is in your way
is always with you too, at least if you got your strength from
football. After you've gotten the beast out of its cage a few times,
using what techniques were required ("You ain't never gonna
play!"), something shifts. After a while, you know that you can
summon the beast, yes. But it also has an inclination to spread
the bars and emerge on its own. Since football, I've had to watch
myself; I've had to be careful of my temper. I've had to let the
Buddhists teach me to breathe deeply, deeply, when there is
something else I might rather do. If I'd had Dickey's success and
Dickey's opportunities I don't know how far the beast might
have run.

Personally, I'll take the bargain. I got more from the game
than I lost—or so I believe. But sometimes it was a close call; I'm
sure of that. Nothing is got for nothing, as the old king says.

In time, I thought that my life in football was over and fully
resolved. But then, thirty years after I swiped my jersey from the
Medford High locker room on Thanksgiving Day 1969, I returned to the game.

I'd sometimes wondered what it would have been like if I
had come to football fully equipped. I did have a few assets. I had
decent physical strength to begin with and added to it quickly.
I had good concentration and I picked up the abstract side of
the game—what's the play? where am I supposed to be?—fast

enough. (Though sometimes I improvised more than I should have.) I had a strong will; it surprised me and everyone I knew how determined I was to make it on the team and play.

But my deficits were multiple. I was way too slow. And my reaction time was terrible—it was as though I had to write myself a mental paragraph on the situation in front of me before I could respond. And of course, I couldn't see: I was the All-Pro Blind-Backer. I didn't have the instinct for the game that some people do. They are always in the right place at the right time; I was almost always not. So I often asked myself: What if I'd come to the game with the same strength of will and the same (relative) intelligence but with physical talent to boot?

Thirty years after the Malden game I walked onto the field again. I was in full pads and helmet, surrounded by all the attendant material: the tackling dummies, the blocking sled, the hollering coaches. And this time I came equipped.

I? Well, that figure on the field, scrunching himself low and then lower at nose tackle, was me and he wasn't. He had my genes, he had my temperament, but he had some other assets as well. It was my son Matthew, the youngest guy on his Pee Wee football team. He played nose tackle, the tough-guy position, though he was at times the smallest kid on the field. Matthew came to football with my will and focus, and something like my level of passion—but he had something else too. My wife, Liz, is a superb athlete—ropewalker's balance, easy coordination; she makes a stroll look like a perfect dream. (I make it look like a job.) In college she was a champ downhill ski racer and she went at it hard. She's broken her leg skiing three times, the last one in a race she entered at close to the age of fifty against women twenty-five years younger. She was (she assures me) winning when the crash came.

Watching Matthew play was like seeing the Jim Brown effect in reverse. When Jim Brown hit the pile of blockers and defenders in front of him, the pile froze; for a second everyone went into suspended animation. One defender came flying off into space, then another. The knot broke and Brown was standing virtually alone—then the gallop downfield.

Matthew was so small in proportion to the other kids on the line that, standing on the side of the field, I often couldn't see him. When the ball snapped, major congestion tended to form around the center; the works gummed up. But then the pile began to move. It began to move backward and sometimes it moved fast. The center fell into the quarterback, who tumbled into the halfback, who got caught up with a guard. It ended in what looked like a massive heap of football laundry five yards in the backfield. At the bottom of that heap: Matthew.

The opposition didn't usually fare much better when its coaches decided to throw a pass. Somehow Matthew always knew when it was going to be a pass. (I never knew what the opposition's play was going to be—after it was blown dead I sometimes could not have told you what it had been.) Matthew had a sort of football ESP. When the quarterback was rolling right, Matthew, having slipped his blocker, was already sliding toward the QB and hunting him down. The QBs were so big in comparison to Matthew that when he did get them it often seemed like he had thrown himself on the side of a tree and was trying to get it to fall over any way he could. Usually the tree fell over.

Sometimes Matthew missed the quarterback on the first try. The QB would leave him ten yards back in the mud. But then Matthew would get into pursuit and run him down. This was something to see. I knew that Matthew was fast but not close to being the fastest kid on his team. When he was chasing someone down, though, he became obscenely fast. And when he caught the guy it wasn't good news. Most Pee Wees tackle with their hands or their arms, or they simply don't tackle at all. Matthew tackled with his shoulder and helmet, and you heard the smack up and down the field.

Midway through his first year, Matthew earned a nickname. He was called T: The Pit Bull. The coaches loved him. Once the head coach gave a talk called "This Is How You Play Football" to the team. In it he described every aspect of Matthew's game: speed (some), muscle, desire, desire, desire. As he talked, he bounced Matthew innocently on his knee. Matthew wasn't in uniform at the time; he was wearing shorts and a T-shirt and the rather owlish metal-framed glasses that he had picked out for himself. To me he looked much as he had when he was a baby. At home, he was serene for a ten-year-old boy. He was kind to his younger brother, William, who is musical and can't see the point of football (Willie referred to the game as fit-ball); Matthew loved his dog; he did his homework, or most of it; he was a pleasure to be with. But on the field he was a terror.

It wasn't only the coach who took an interest in Matthew. Howie Long did too. Howie Long, as the football world knows, is one of the star commentators on FOX's NFL show. Before that he was a football great, playing for the Oakland Raiders and making his way to the Super Bowl. Watching Howie Long go after a quarterback was like watching a tornado that had developed intelligence and had a particular object of destruction in mind. I remember a brilliant maneuver where he got low, swung toward the sideline, then steamrollered the blocker onto his back. Howie played with a certain intensity: Once after what he took to be a dismal effort on his part against the Houston Oilers, he woke up the next morning still in a rage with himself. To express his feelings, he took his uniform out behind his hotel, dropped it in a heap, soaked it in kerosene, and set it on fire. He made it into the Hall of Fame, though he was said to be undersized for a D-lineman.

A son of his was on Matthew's team; Howie was frequently around for practice and turned up at a surprising number of games. Standing close to Howie Long, as I did occasionally on the sideline, I can attest that he did not look undersized. He looked like a member of another species—related to humans, but larger, stronger, far less destructible. Howie also looks smarter and more invested with probity than most of us. His forehead is unusually high; his jaw strong; his eyes, behind wire-rimmed, slightly professorial glasses, steady. If you got onto Mount Rushmore based on appearance alone, Howie Long would have it locked. When Howie talks, it seems as though the world ought to listen.

At least I did. He and I actually didn't speak much at all—a few sentences from time to time. But when we did, Howie usually said something generously admiring about my son, the Pit Bull. "That kid is super tough." "The boy knows how to tackle." Those are two that I remember. Howie said this! Howie Long! Not merely someone who had played football and starred. But someone who was what they call an NFL legend—and also someone who continued on as a media star, one of America's commanding voices on the subject of football. Howie Long admired my kid's game.

Well, talk about redemption! I had won my football laurels. I had maybe won them a little late, but I had won them. And sure, the accolades were a bit indirect—they came not really to me but to my son. But he was *mine*. He carried my genes. And I coached him all the time. We talked constantly about how he could improve his game. We had wonderful conversations going to practice and coming back.

At home we watched games together, the way my father and I had done. We delighted in the hard hits. Wham! Blast! Smack! With every blow we hollered our appreciation. By watching, Matthew learned more about the game—he learned better how to tackle, how to throw an oversize quarterback down. He learned how to outmaneuver an especially tough blocker. (How many other Pee Wee ballplayers in America used the swim move?) He learned to read his opponent and tailor his game to what he read. "If he's strong, use your quickness," I told him. "If he's quick, run him over."

"What if he's both?" Matthew asked.

"No one," I told him, "is going to be as strong *and* as quick as you are."

My father wasn't in the room with us, at least not physically. He died early, in his fifties, a decade before Matthew was born. But if he'd been there, I can imagine what he might have said. "Forget the instruction. Leave the swim move to the coaches," he might have told me. "Tell him about Jim Brown. Tell him about Tittle—yeah, mostly Tittle. Tell him how the guy built himself up a piece at a time. Tell him about Tittle. And when you have a sec, go grab me a pack of Camels. I'm out of cigareets." But I told Matthew none of that. I told him how he (and I) could shine on the field.

I had read some books on parenting. I had heard rumors about how you shouldn't use your child to compensate for past failures. I understood that it was a bad idea to try to get your son to redeem your old faults. But as I saw it, I wasn't bending Matthew against his will. He *loved* to play football. He told me over and over that football practice was the best part of his day. And I wasn't one of those truly insane football dads. I wasn't like Stan's father. Stan was a defensive tackle and when the ball was snapped, his father crushed his hands into massive rocks, raised them up beside his ears, and cried out, "Damn it, Stan, hit somebody!"

I became something of a celebrity with the other dads: My son was the Pit Bull. He was the only kid on the field who really seemed to enjoy delivering a good thwack. When the dads found out that I was a college professor, they were incredulous. "A professor? And you're the Pit Bull's father, right?" Naturally I found observations like this highly gratifying. I always had someone to talk to at the team barbecues. One dad invited me to go squirrel hunting with him.

I knew that you're not supposed to use your kids to compensate for your shortcomings. That doesn't work. It blows up in your face. But the thing was, on this particular occasion—this one-in-a-million time—it *was* working. Howie Long! Barbecues! Squirrel hunting! Matthew loved football. He was great at it. I loved that he was great at it, and it made me feel better about a host of failings that I didn't know I had felt bad about.

Matthew's team won a couple of championships. He got bigger and stronger and faster and moved to defensive end. No one ran sweeps to his side; no one ran near him. In the final game of his last season he stepped back into the middle guard spot for a goal-line stand. The other team was on the one-yard line. It was first down. If Matthew's team stopped them, the game was over—time to get the trophies and go home. (Was the losing team going to get trophies too? No, I live in the South.) His team stopped them four times; Matthew made three of the tackles.

In between plays he went up and down the line, exhorting the troops in ways that would have put Patton to shame. They won—he won—the trophy came home.

And soon Matthew stopped playing. He went out for his high school team, he got hurt, he came back. But you could see his heart wasn't in it. Once driving home from a scrimmage I asked him what was up. The atmosphere was somehow very clear on that drive back, the way it can get between a father and son when both are tired and a little tipsy with the fatigue. He told me first that he was getting sick of being screamed at by half-cracked coaches. It wasn't hard to see his point: He did have some screamers coaching him (I thought of my own coach going on about Johnny and about the "punch in the mouth" rant), and they were probably not the best football minds in America.

"Also," he said, "I'm not really mad anymore."

"Mad?"

"Yeah, when I was being Pit Bull, I was really mad."

"But not anymore?"

"Not really."

It turned out that what he was mad about was having to go off to a reading tutor certain days after school. School at the time was torture and the reading tutor was torture on top. We thought Matthew wasn't reading fast enough or well enough, given what seemed (and turned out to be) extraordinary intelligence. So we submitted him to assault-phonics three times a week. He hated it. But instead of complaining, or complaining much, he threw his ten-year-old's passion (which can be formidable enough) into football. Many quarterbacks and running backs paid for that phonics abuse, and quite a few small centers and guards suffered too.

Does family history have to repeat? Thirty years before on a football field I'd revved myself up with my humiliation mantra. "You ain't never gonna play!" I don't know what my son was whispering to himself as he roared into the backfield, but it may not have been all that different.

Matthew acquired some valuable qualities playing ball, but he probably paid for them too, just as I did. For football is what Plato calls a pharmakon, a poison and an elixir. Football can do great good: build the body, create a stronger, more resilient will, impart confidence, stimulate bravery, and cultivate loyalty. If I hadn't played football, my life would have been different and (I'm nearly sure) poorer than it has been. I'm certain that I'm not the only guy in America who can say that.

But football is a dangerous game. The chance of concussion is constant; the repercussions last for a long time. The chance of maiming your body isn't small, either. If you play high-power college ball, you may well have physical pain from it for the rest of your life. If you play pro ball, you almost surely will. Part of the reason that Howie Long is so ramrod straight and dignified-looking is that he has trouble moving his neck.

But the dangers of football go beyond physical risk. There is risk to the spirit as well. You can lose more than you gain by being a football player, and the losses aren't trivial. Football can brutalize a man. It can make him more aggressive, even violent.

Too many football players devolve into brutes. Is football courage really courage—or is it all about compensation? Sometimes I almost believe that every great ballplayer is a raging Achilles. Does noble Hector, the guy who can turn it off when he needs to, even exist?

The game can make a player intolerant of gentleness. It can help turn him into a member of a pack that mistreats and even scapegoats others—the weak, the differently made. The game can make men unthinking; their football-based character often seals them off from real reflection. They seem to talk and even to think like machines. (I owe it all to my teammates. I just followed the game plan. We do it for the fans.) Football can encourage illusions about war and heroism. The game's relation to America's racial politics is distressing to contemplate. And football's merger with religion, especially Christianity, isn't far short of ridiculous. Does Jesus really care if Medford beats Everett?

Football is a pharmakon. The game gives and the game takes away and it does so for high stakes. Its potential benefits are vast; its dangers are too. And football may be the most potent form of education that America now offers. Melville famously said that a whaling ship was his university, his Harvard and his Yale. How many of us now are being educated by football? How many of us celebrate the gains it can bring—wonderful as they are—without calibrating the costs? There's much more to the game than the coaches say. Football educates for good and for ill, and it's important to remember that from time to time. I can't tell you where my undergrad diploma is, and my grad diploma, which was pretty grand-looking, got lost in a move. But in the bottom drawer of my dresser, there's my football jersey, Medford Mustangs, number 66, white and rich royal blue. It's the one that I swiped from the locker room on Thanksgiving Day 1969. (Somehow it still carries the stain from the dunk in that mud puddle.) I get a look at that jersey nearly every day.

ACKNOWLEDGMENTS

Strong gratitude and great good wishes to my editor, Scott Moyers, who knew there was a book for me on this subject well before I did and helped in numberless ways to make it happen. Thanks too to those who read the manuscript through and aided me with their thoughts: That's Scott; and Michael Pollan; my agent, Chris Calhoun; and my son Matthew Denton-Edmundson, who has learned much of what his father has to teach about writing and is now doing some teaching in return. Warm thanks to the staff at Penguin for doing so much to get this manuscript into shape and ready for the world: gratitude to Akif Saifi, Veronica Windholz, and Kym Surridge.

Thanks for her graciousness to Nancy Miller at Bloomsbury, and for help at the inception from Jean Tamarin and Liz McMillen, at *The Chronicle Review*. Thanks also to Jahan Ramazani, Michael DeLeo, John Aquino, Margaret Costa, Elizabeth Wallace, Mike Kelley, Gordon Matthew, Cindy Wall, and David Mikics, who, sometimes knowingly, sometimes not, gave me valuable assistance along the way. And thanks to my long-lost cousin, Jeff—the Hawk—Hawkins, director of football operations at the University of Oregon, who shone a beam inside the world of big-time college ball.

I'm grateful to Mike London, Jerry Capone, Steve Fairchild, the other coaches, and the players for the University of Virginia football team. They graciously let me into their football lives and answered my questions. I'm grateful too to UVA athletic director Craig Littlepage for opening the door for me. Thanks to the authors of the stack of football books I've read. In particular I'm grateful to (and recommend) Ray Blount Jr. for *About Three Bricks Shy of a Load*, H. G. Bissinger for *Friday Night Lights*, and Jim Brown for his two volumes of autobiography. I also profited from Spike Lee's movie about Brown: *Jim Brown: All-American*. Thanks too to audiences at Monterey Bay Community College (and especially to my marvelous host, David Clemens) and at Princeton University for listening to my talks about football and asking tough questions.

This book, as the Yankee sage would put it, is déjà vu all over again, my having written about these years before, from a different angle and through another lens. Memory shifts and glides and swims and (sometimes) fades; I've tried to stay true to events as I recall them here and now. People tell me that my powers of recollection are keen enough. But that doesn't mean they're perfect—far from it. Others may recall matters differently. This book is my truth, the way it was for me. I'm grateful to have known all those who appear in these pages and I feel only affection for them. Still, it seems right to hide all but my family members and the well-known (there were few enough of those in Medford, Massachusetts, circa '69) beneath fabricated names and now and then a changed physique.

Finally my family: Thanks to Matthew for being himself, and thanks to my son Willie, guitarist and singer extraordinaire, who supplied the sound track to the writing of this book. Gratitude in the extreme to my brother, Phil, always behind my books and me. Thanks last to my wife, Liz, who is a bit less fascinated with football than I am but whose love and friendship over thirty-five years made this venture possible.